Family Handbook

of

Christian Knowledge

THE CREATION

Family Handbook

of

Christian Knowledge

THE CREATION

Editor

JOSH McDOWELL

Written by

DON STEWART

CAMPUS CRUSADE FOR CHRIST

Published by

HERE'S LIFE PUBLISHERS, INC.

San Bernardino, California 92402

Family Handbook of Christian Knowledge: THE CREATION
Edited by Josh McDowell
Written by Don Stewart

A Campus Crusade for Christ Book
Published by
HERE'S LIFE PUBLISHERS, INC.
P. O. Box 1576
San Bernardino, CA 92402

ISBN 0-86605-118-X
Library of Congress Catalogue Card 83-072898
HLP Product No. 403139
© 1984 by Campus Crusade for Christ, Inc.
All rights reserved.

Adapted from the book originally written by
Willem J. J. Glashouwer and Willem J. Ouweneel,
and published in Dutch under the title:
    "Het ontstaan van de Wereld"
    Published by Stichting "De Evangelische Omroep"
        Oude Amersfoortseweg 79a
        1200 AN HILVERSUM
        The Netherlands
    Originally published in 1980.
Unless otherwise indicated, Scripture quotations are from the New American Standard Bible, copyright The Lockman Foundation 1960, 1962, 1963, 1968, 1971, 1972, 1973, 1975, and are used by permission.

FOR MORE INFORMATION, WRITE:
L.I.F.E. P.O. Box A399, Sydney South 2000, Australia
Campus Crusade for Christ of Canada Box 368, Abbottsford, B.C., V25 4N9, Canada
Campus Crusade for Christ 103 Friar Street, Reading RG1 1EP, Berkshire, England
Lay Institute for Evangelism P.O. Box 8786, Auckland 3, New Zealand
Great Commission Movement of Nigeria P.O. Box 500, Jos, Plateau State, Nigeria, West Africa
Life Ministry P.O. Box/Bus 91015, Auckland Park 2006, Republic of So. Africa
Campus Crusade for Christ Int'l Arrowhead Springs, San Bernardino, CA 92414, U.S.A.

TABLE OF CONTENTS

INTRODUCTION

The Creation is one of five volumes of the *Family Handbook of Christian Knowledge*. In the first volume we discussed the Bible as God's Word. We saw that the Bible, composed of sixty-six books divided into Old and New Testaments, is God's perfect and revealed Word to mankind. We briefly discussed several ideas pertaining to the Bible's inspiration. We explored its history, noting its various authors, the long time-period over which it was written, the different types of inspired books included in it, and its historical, scientific, and religious accuracy.

The scope of the Bible includes the history of all creation. The first book of the Bible, Genesis, describes the beginning of all things—when God "spoke forth" the universe and its component parts. The last book of the Bible, Revelation, describes the final state of all things, a future world beyond our furthest human expectations, a world possible only through the dynamic power of God. These five volumes will survey that vast history.

In *The Creation* we are ready to look at the Bible's account of the beginning of time—creation itself. Our concern is with origins. How did the universe begin? Has it always been there? Is it an illusion? If it had a beginning, what sort of beginning was it? We will use the Genesis account of creation as the basis for our study, but we also will delve into related areas of philosophy and science. We will see that the Genesis account of creation, far from being an ancient and fanciful myth, is an accurate, historical summary of the original creation of this universe and all that is in it.

Because much of secular science presupposes that there is no God, no design, no creative pattern, we will discuss those ideas. We will show the harmony between true scientific evidence (not just scientific interpretation or speculation) and the Genesis account. Also, since much secular science is preoccupied with the theory of evolution (the view that all contemporary life forms evolved from earlier, more simple life forms), a significant portion of our handbook will deal with evolution.

Our purpose is to acquaint Christian readers with Christian knowledge in a broad way. These are not meant to be definitive textbooks on the various subjects broached. However, the material presented is accurate and is based on a much broader framework of research and study. Therefore, although we will discuss philosophical ideas about the origin and nature of the universe, we will not present complicated philosophical arguments. We will discuss theories of origins, but we will not engage in comprehensive surveys of scientific data. We will provide a framework for analyzing and assessing evolutionary theories in the light of biblical revelation, but we will not presume to set forth thorough argumentation in each of the areas under debate. We are confident that this book will equip Christian families with the tools necessary to defend their Christian commitment against contemporary secular scientific and philosophic thought.

It should be noted that the author is addressing these issues from certain perspectives. He believes in a universal flood and leans toward, though is not necessarily convinced by, the recent creationist view (that is, the earth is much younger than the 4-7 billion years that modern science needs in order to hold an evolutionary point of view). There are good Christian scholars, both scientific and biblical, who would differ from his perspective and would argue for a local flood or an old earth or for a progressive creationism. It must be understood clearly that there is room for a difference of opinion here and the author does not consider either view the "Christian" view. Both are viable options. However it is beyond the scope of this book to deal with all the arguments for and against the age of the earth and the extent of the flood. Bible-believing Christians can disagree upon these issues; however, one thing we all agree upon is that the universe came into existence by a series of creative acts by an infinite, personal God.

Travel with us, then, as we go back past recorded history to the beginning of it all—to the time when God, the Eternal King, first created everything through the power of His Word.

CHAPTER ONE

Science and Society Grow Away From God

While the Bible is not a science text, we can trust the Bible to tell us the truth about the universe around us. God gave us the universe, the stars, the sun, and our earth. He has also given us His Word in the Bible.

Above right: René Descartes was a Christian and a philosopher. His philosophical arguments for the existence of God had a profound effect on the development of scientific methodology.

Why does the sun look red as it sets? Why is the world the way we see it? Where did human beings come from? Why are we here? Is there something or someone outside our universe who caused it? As long as there have been humans on earth, there have been minds questioning the world around them.

We humans have been especially interested in origins, in the *whys* of our universe (those *whys* sometimes are called philosophical questioning). This book will show the biblical perspective on the *whys* and *hows* of the origin of the universe. Using primarily the first eleven chapters of the Old Testament book of Genesis, we will explore these questions and the secular and biblical answers to them.

A seventeenth-century French philosopher, René Descartes (1596-1650), asked: "How do we establish the reality of our own existence?" In the Christian era, and up to the time of Descartes, philosophy and science were generally affiliated with tenets of the church. In contrast, Descartes attempted to develop a philosophical system, based solely on mathematical principles, which he felt would give absolute certainty. His system would differ from those of his contemporaries by its clarity and certitude. The basis of his system was that even doubt about one's own existence could bring certainty of that existence. If one doubts that he exists, he must exist, because there must be *someone* doing the doubting. Descartes coined a phrase which has become famous: *"Cogito ergo sum"* ("I think, therefore, I am"). Descartes was not irreligious; he believed in revelation and even attempted to prove God's existence through his system. He was, however, the forerunner of other philosophers who built their systems apart from assumptions of God's existence.

Descartes was one of many philosophers from the Middle Ages through the Renaissance and Reformation, who profoundly shaped the

The great Catholic theologian of the Middle Ages, Thomas Aquinas, asserted two realms of knowledge: reason and revelation. Aquinas' systematic theology is still important in Roman Catholic and even Protestant defenses of the existence of God.

relationship between religion/faith and science/reason. From seeds sown in the Middle Ages, through the growth of independent thought during the Renaissance and Reformation, science and reason blossomed into the flower of scientific thought apart from God in the later Enlightenment.

Thomas Aquinas (1225-1274) was one of the most influential philosophers of the Middle Ages. A Roman Catholic, his ideas nevertheless paved the way for much later thought that diverged sharply from Roman Catholic catechisms. He is best known for his magnificent and intellectually challenging arguments for the existence of God. He was a great philosophical champion for the biblical God. Ever since his time, philosophical and religious leaders have revered Aquinas as a superb thinker and apologist for the faith. Even today the Roman Catholic church bases a great deal of its philosophical argumentation on the works of Aquinas.

Aquinas separated the two fields of philosophy and theology. To him, philosophy has as its domain everything that is open to argumentation. The purpose of philosophy is to establish objective truth that can be discovered by the use of human reason. Theology, on the other hand, has revealed truth, or faith, as its domain. Reason is incapable of discovering or demonstrating revelation or theology.

But, Aquinas was quick to point out, those two fields overlap, since no truth can contradict any other truth. For example, Aquinas saw the existence of God as both reasonable and revealed. It is possible to discover the existence of God through philosophy, through reason. It is also true that one can discover the existence of God through revelation. There is no conflict between the two. (Of course, some of the attributes and actions of this God are outside the domain of philosophy and it remains for theology to reveal them. Although the two fields are overlapping, they are not identical.)

Above: Galileo believed that the world around us could be studied without religious presuppositions or bias. Because his system was so different from that of his scientific colleagues, they urged the Roman Catholic Church to censure him for heresy.
Right: The work of Aquinas, Descartes, and others revolutionized scientific, philosophical, and theological thought. That revolution is symbolized by the procession of the Goddess of Reason through the streets of Paris during the French Revolution.

The groundwork Aquinas' philosophy laid for the later growth of science away from God lay in his early distinction between philosophy (using reason) and theology (using revelation). Later philosophers and scientists took that theme, erased the overlap, and developed a new scientific system that did not take theology or God into account.

Various prominent thinkers after Aquinas also contributed to that groundwork. The scientist Galileo (1564-1642) is not remembered primarily for his contributions to philosophy, but for his scientific views and the resultant persecution he suffered. What was revolutionary about Galileo's scientific findings was that they were based on scientific observation, from which he then developed his philosophical framework. Until Galileo most scientists were philosophers first; they began

The different perspectives on the universe assumed in the West and in Russia are illustrated by noting that the American astronauts on Apollo 8 read Genesis 1 while in orbit on Christmas Eve, while Russian cosmonaut G. Titov declared in 1961, "I did not see God." Below: Copernicus postulated a heliocentric universe rather than the commonly accepted view that the earth was the center of the universe.

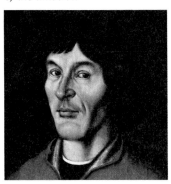

with their philosophical world view and then used scientific observation to confirm that world view. Galileo's thinking was revolutionary for his day. He proposed that scientific observation itself provided the only reliable philosophical world view. Using his own newly modified telescope (although not an instrument he had invented), he *observed* that the moon had craters and mountains. He concluded that since it did have such "imperfections," his philosophical world view would have to be modified to account for them. Other philosopher/scientists had developed their world view with the presupposition that all heavenly bodies must literally and physically imitate the perfections of the Lord God and so must in themselves be perfectly spherical. Their tendency was to dismiss Galileo's observations as untrustworthy, not on empirical grounds, but because they contradicted the accepted philosophical viewpoint.

It was because of this philosophical debate that the church got into the argument. While the church itself was not against science or against Galileo personally, the philosophers claimed that Galileo's method (trusting observation *first*) attacked the basis of biblical theology. Given the philosophical climate of the day it is understandable that the church, with its great power, sided with the philosopher/scientists and censured Galileo. The *Encyclopaedia Britannica* discussed the influence

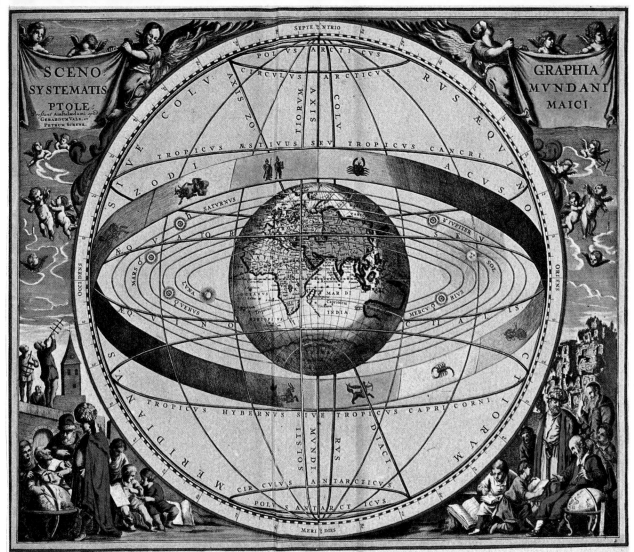

The seventeeth century chart illustrates the Alexandrian astronomer Ptolemy's geocentric view of the universe. Ptolemy lived ca. A.D. 85-160.

the scientists had on the actions of the Church against Galileo:

"The Aristotelian professors, seeing their vested interests threatened, united against him. They strove to cast suspicion upon him in the eyes of ecclesiastical authorities because of contradictions between the Copernican theory, and the Scriptures. They obtained cooperation of the Dominican preachers, who fulminated from the pulpit against the new impiety of mathematicians and secretly denounced Galileo to the Inquisition for blasphemous utterances, which, they said, he had freely invented."[1]

Years later the church's position gave way to the Enlightenment's adoption of Galileo's system. And the Enlightenment went much further than religious Galileo intended, by installing *reason* as supreme over all. Still, Galileo's emphasis on empirical scientific method was a keystone in building the "science-without-God" edifice.

Here we come to a thesis of this book. A reasonable interpretation of the evidence and a reasonable interpretation of Scripture will result in no conflict between the two. If the God who created the universe and its contents also created the message of the Bible, should it be any wonder that each of them testifies to the same truth?

Do Science and Scripture Really Conflict?

From this brief look at Descartes, Aquinas and Galileo we can see the germ of some of the patterns that later gradually pushed science and theology apart. Today many people firmly believe that the two disciplines are mutually exclusive, completely contradictory to each other. Aquinas made a distinction between theology and science. Galileo emphasized the priority of scientific observation over philosophical speculation. Descartes founded his philosophy on mathematical reasoning rather than on revealed theology. Each of these men's major ideas, although not inherently anti-Christian or anti-God, contributed to the Enlightenment's eventual rejection of God, the Bible, and even religion itself.

That rejection, however, was not necessary. That kind of polarization is artificial. It is not required either by scientific fact or by biblical truth. If

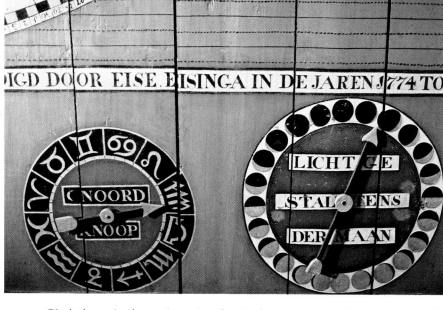

Dutch astronomer Eise Eisinga built a planetarium in Franeker, Holland, between 1774 and 1781. The models within reflect the orderly movement of the heavenly bodies precisely enough that it still functions as an accurate representation of the heavens.

we as Christians believe that the God of creation is also the God of salvation, then such conflict is impossible. The same God will not create one testimony in the material record of the universe and then create a completely contradictory testimony in the written record of the Bible. Theologian Bernard Ramm comments:

"God cannot contradict His speech in Nature by His speech in Scripture. If the Author of Nature and Scripture are the same God, then the two books of God must eventually recite the same story. Therefore, in place of resentment or suspicion or vilification toward science and scientists, we must have a spirit of respect and gratitude. In place of a narrow hyperdogmatic attitude toward science we are to be careful, reserved, openminded. We are to pay due respect to *both* science and Scripture. Neither adoration of one nor bigoted condemnation of the other is correct. We must be ready to hear the voice of science and the voice of Scripture on common matters. The spirit of mutual respect for *both* science and Scripture preserves us from any charge of being anti-scientific or blindly dogmatic or superstitious in our religious beliefs as they pertain to Nature."[2]

We do not want to return to the scientifically naive world view of those like Ptolemy (ca. A.D. 85-160), who philosophically perceived the universe as being *geo*-centric — that is, with the earth at the center of all existence. Neither do we want to abandon geocentricism with the idea that to do so is to abandon the Bible. The Bible nowhere teaches that the earth is the center of the universe. The Bible, although accurate in the little science it does broach, is not primarily concerned with science but with salvation. The location of the earth in relationship to the rest of the universe is irrelevant when compared to the spiritual concerns of the Bible. As we shall see in this volume, there is no ultimate conflict between the reasonable and objective observation and interpretation of data (science) and a reasonable and objective interpretation of the Bible (theology).

The Crab nebula in the constellation Taurus is evidence of a star which exploded in 1054. Such signs of disorder or catastrophe in the universe are not evidence against the general order or design of the universe.

From a biblical perspective, the story of the relationship of God and mankind is at the center of all existence. The Bible is concerned primarily with our relationship to God, not with a scientific model of the universe. Quite properly, then, the Bible deals extensively with moral and philosophical ideas and only incidentally mentions scientific topics. That is not a new view of the Bible and science. Even Galileo recognized the different (but sometimes overlapping) fields of science and the Bible. Biographer Stillman Drake described Galileo's view like this:

"The Bible was quite a different matter. No contradiction of Holy Scripture could be permitted in science, any more than in other things. Fortunately the apparent contradictions between astronomy and the Bible were few in number, since the Bible did not attempt to teach astronomy as did the philosophers....Science could not proceed independently of the expert theological opinion, but agreement between them could easily be assured."[3]

As we shall see in the following chapters, the few biblical passages that appear to contradict science in no way contradict reasonably interpreted and accurately observed scientific data. We shall see that the primary "conflict" between science and the Bible is in reality a conflict between antisupernatural presuppositions of scientists and the theistic, and thus supernatural, assertions of the Bible.

Testimony of the Stars

Science has much to offer the committed Christian. The observations of modern science can contribute greatly to our understanding of the universe, which we believe was created by and is sustained by the God of the Bible.

Science has come a long way since earliest recorded history. In just the last four hundred years, since the primitive modified telescopes of Galileo, the study of the stars (astronomy) has developed at an astonishing rate. Galileo's discovery of mountains and craters on the moon, for example, was incredible in his day. Yet today astronomers

Right: Charles Darwin's general theory of evolution revolutionized the scientific study of life and its origins. Sigmund Freud's theory of psychotherapy revolutionized the scientific study of man.
Below: Karl Marx's atheistic social and political theories revolutionized political study and action. All three "revolutionaries" advanced atheistic control of science.

have developed complex techniques for seeing millions of stars invisible to the unaided eye. In addition to today's much improved telescope, they use sophisticated apparatus to measure the size of stars, their distance from the earth and from each other, and their rate of travel. They even estimate stellar age and composition.

Of course, scientists are not unanimous in their interpretation of data. For example, it might seem at first glance that all scientists are agreed on the basic interpretations of these astronomical data. That is not necessarily true, especially when the evidence is fragmentary or inconclusive. We must make clear, however, that the data do not contradict or automatically provide an interpretation. The data are just a record of what someone has observed. To make sense of data, one must interpret data. And it is in this area of science that scientists disagree, for a variety of reasons. For example, using the same tools and recognizing the same data, scientists still are sharply divided over the facts of the origin of the universe.

Astronomers look at "red shift" evidence in determining the speed with which galaxies move. The evidence is there. But what does it mean? To some scientists, the evidence seems compatible with an eternal universe that is in an expanding period of its continual oscillation. To other scientists, the evidence seems compatible with a universe that began in chaos and darkness. Even those scientists who believe that the universe had a beginning cannot agree on the cause of that beginning. Thus, scientists do not usually disagree about the evidence (providing, of course, that the evidence has been confirmed through recognized scientific method). They disagree about its proper interpretation. As we shall discover in this book, the world view of the Bible is not at variance with scientific evidence. It is at variance with some scientific interpretations, which are in themselves world views, and which oppose the world view of the Bible. We will show that an objective and reasonable interpretation of scientific data will be compatible with rather than controvert the biblical record.

Above: The title page of Descartes' book (1637), wherein his system of rational philosophical thought was described. His emphasis on reason as sufficient by itself to determine truth allowed the later development of the assumption of reason without God.

Right: Karl Marx recognized the similarities between his political presuppositions and Darwin's scientific presuppositions. He sent Darwin an autographed copy of Das Kapital.

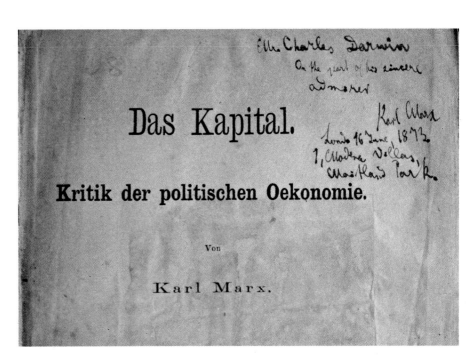

A Scientific World View Without God

The contemporary "scientific" world view is a world view that has completely abandoned any belief in God. There are several reasons for the rejection of God by science after the centuries during which belief in God and His ordered universe was the anchor on which religious scientists depended in identifying and understanding that order. Three thinkers in the nineteenth century represent some of the bias against religion that helped to oust God from the scientific world view.

Charles Darwin (1809-1882) revolutionized the biological sciences. Rather than evidentially or presuppositionally accepting the special creation of all earthly life by God, Darwin instead chose to observe a vast quantity of biological data. From that he developed a theory of its origin based on naturalism (rather than allowing for any supernatural intervention).

He proposed that organisms change and develop in fundamental complexity through adaptation and natural selection from one species to another or within species. The key to his system was that the changes were by adaptation and natural selection. There was no need for God in this system of change. In fact, Darwin was an atheist and his view of the origin of life fit his atheistic world view. Darwin's interpretation of his data, however, was not as far-reaching and all-encompassing as today's evolutionary model. When later scientists expanded Darwin's theory to include the development and origin of all life over a vast period of time, the agency and ultimate source for this evolution was chance, not God. We will discuss Darwin and his theory to a greater extent in chapters four and five.

Karl Marx (1818-1883) revolutionized political science and sociology. Until his time, although many people had differing ideas about God, most political science, economics, and social structures depended on some sort of assumed or explicit divine absolute for their structure and values. Marx, however, was atheistic. He viewed belief in God as a

While many religions make claims but can provide no substantiation of their claims by history or science, Christianity is based in and confirmed by history and evidence. The resurrection of Jesus Christ was an historical, verifiable event. He was buried in and rose again from a tomb very much like (if not identical to) the well-known Garden Tomb in Jerusalem.

hindrance to economic, political, and social development. He did not orient his system around any divine absolute. Instead, he proposed a political system (communism) oriented around the impersonal and arbitrary absolute of dialectical materialism. There was not only no need for God in Marx's system, any idea of God was detrimental to human progress.[4]

Sigmund Freud (1856-1939) revolutionized the social sciences through his unique form of psychology, called psychoanalysis. Freud was a forerunner of social scientists who orient their therapy and values subjectively, abandoning the concept that right and wrong are objectively and absolutely determined by God. Right and wrong, indeed all morals and values, become subjective and relative. Psychotherapy did not have as its goal the reconciliation of the individual to the laws of God, which previously was seen as the path to personal happiness. Rather, Freud's psychotherapy had as its goal the reconciliation of the individual's facets of personality to each other. With the advent of relativistic therapy and values (ethics), Freud and his followers believed they had no need for God.

These three thinkers of the last century and many of their contemporaries are now gone. Their influence, however, has pervaded every facet of modern science. Contemporary science is a science without God, without absolutes and, as we shall see in subsequent chapters, without adequate answers to the *whys* and *hows* of the universe and of mankind.

Partnership Between Faith and Evidence

The *whys* and *hows* of the universe and mankind are answered by the revelation of the Lord God in the Bible and in His Son, Jesus Christ. Hebrews 1:1-2 declares, "God, after He spoke long ago to the fathers in the prophets in many portions and in many ways, in these last days has spoken to us in His Son." Contrary to the antisupernaturalists, there is no absolute contradiction between the Bible and the evidence of science. There is, in fact, a partnership between faith and evidence. This partnership is illustrated in the book of Hebrews: "Now faith is the assurance of things hoped for, the conviction of things not seen....By faith we understand that the worlds were prepared by the word of God, so that what is seen was not made out of things which are visible."[5] The following chapters in this volume describe the partnership between faith and evidence mentioned by the writer of Hebrews. We will find that faith, as described in the Bible, complements and is confirmed by the evidence we find in reality around us.

The entire Christian faith, the gospel of truth, couples faith and evidence. The apostle Paul defined the gospel as the death, burial, and resurrection of Jesus Christ.[6] He declared that faith and evidence were so closely related that "if Christ has not been raised, your faith is worthless; you are still in your sins."[7] The tomb was empty. The angel testified that its occupant had risen.[8] That was the consistent theme of the New Testament writers as they preached the gospel (the word means *good news*) and defended their faith.

The apostle Peter preached the first recorded evangelistic message after the resurrection of Christ. In it he pointed to the evidence. He pointed to the world of reality to confirm the reality of the resurrection of Jesus Christ. Peter appealed to the knowledge of his listeners: "Men of Israel, listen to these words: Jesus the Nazarene, a man *attested to you* by God with miracles and wonders and signs which God performed through Him *in your midst, just as you yourselves know—*....This Jesus God raised up again, to which *we are all witnesses.*"[9] Later he emphasized the corroborating value of evidence in his first epistle: "For we did not follow cleverly devised tales when we made known to you the power and coming of our Lord Jesus Christ, but *we were eyewitnesses* of His majesty."[10]

The apostle Paul was one of the most intellectual and philosophical of the early Christians. Some of his arguments in defense of the faith have been presesrved for us in the New Testament. From them we can see Paul's emphasis on the use of reason, evidence, and common sense in testing and understanding reality. One of Paul's greatest speeches (of those that have been preserved for us in the New Testament) was before some Greek philosophers on Mars Hill in Athens (Acts 17). When Paul arrived in a new place he always began preaching the gospel of Jesus Christ in the Jewish synagogue. Then he also preached the gospel in the area marketplace or anywhere else he was sure to find a crowd to talk

When the apostles preached the gospel, they pointed to the evidence for the resurrection of Jesus Christ to substantiate the claims of Christianity. The classic Beato Angelico illustrates one of Christ's post-resurrection appearances— to Mary in the garden. He admonished her, "Do not cling to Me."

to. When he came to the synagogue of the Jews in Thessalonica, the Scripture records that "he went to them, and for three Sabbaths *reasoned* with them from the Scriptures, *explaining and giving evidence* that the Christ had to suffer and rise again from the dead, and saying, 'This Jesus whom I am proclaiming to you is the Christ.'"[11]

The same chapter records Paul's actions in Athens. It says that since he was "provoked within him as he was beholding the city full of idols,"[12] he was "*reasoning* in the synagogue with the Jews and the God-fearing Gentiles, and in the marketplace every day with those who happened to be present."[13] Some of the Greek philosophers observed Paul preaching in this manner and invited him to address their gathering. Paul's speech is one of the greatest short summations asserting the existence of God and the gospel of Jesus Christ.[14]

What Paul had to say about "science" is interesting too. Many anti-supernaturalists would like to believe that the New Testament concept of God is primitive, that the biblical God's creative agency is vastly inferior to a complex naturalistic scientific model. But the Creator God asserted by Paul in Acts 17 is very sophisticated; His creative act fits modern scientific evidence much better than do the myths of the crude Greek deities. Paul called his God, "the God who made the world and all things in it,... Lord of heaven and earth [not dwelling] in temples made with hands; neither is He served by human hands, as though He needed anything, since He Himself gives to all life and breath and all things."[15] As we shall see in this volume, the God of the Bible, the God proclaimed by and revealed fully in Jesus Christ, has a far better explanation for the origin of the universe than does modern atheistic "science." The range of science, both ancient and modern, sophisticated and primitive, is vast. From the ancient "three-storied universe" models, through Babylonian epic myths, through the record of God's Word in the Bible, through the intricate systems of Isaac Newton and his contemporaries, to the vast system we call science today, the God described by the writer of Hebrews "upholds all things by the word of His power."[16] This is the God who produced our universe and who sustains it today. This is the God who explains the *whys* and *hows* of our existence in the person of our Lord and Savior Jesus Christ.[17]

Today we send vehicles throughout our solar system. Astronauts travel through outer space on almost a routine basis. We depend on the many satellites circling our globe to provide us with weather information, news events, telecommunications, sports events, and entertainment. Since the first space ventures in the 1950s, our knowledge of the universe has multiplied a thousandfold. And yet we still cannot demonstrate or explain scientifically the origin of the universe. The question of origins, long discussed among philosophers and theologians, is unanswered by science alone, even the advanced, complicated, physics-oriented science of the end of the twentieth century.

Certainly science can tell us a great deal about the world we live in and about our relationship to that world. There was no real academic discipline as we know science during most of mankind's history. Most ancient (sometimes described as primitive) societies pictured the world in religious terms rather than in scientific terms.

Is the universe really here, or is it an illusion? Why is there something rather than nothing? Why am I here? How and when did everything start? Is there order and design in the universe, or is everything random, the result of chance? Properly, questions such as these belong in the fields of philosophy or religion. Science, however, can be used as a tool to point toward answers for some of them. Science *describes;* it does not justify what it describes. However, as we shall see, the universe science describes is a universe that reflects order, design, personal creative agency, and purpose. Scientific evidence points toward a Creator much like the God of the Bible. Respected astronomer and self-proclaimed agnostic Robert Jastrow observed that science presupposes principles upon which it is based, almost like the way religious believers presuppose some religious tenets. He said, "There is a kind of religion in science; it is the religion of a person who believes there is order and harmony in the Universe. Every event can be explained in a rational way as the product of some previous event; every effect must have its cause."[18]

Left: Christianity is a religion distinct from all other religions and the Christian God is distinct from all other gods. This painting by Arazzo Raffaellesco illustrates the apostle Paul's convincing declaration of God and the gospel to the pagan Athenian philosophers (Acts 17:23-27).

Although science really never can answer the questions we have posed above, it can illustrate some pictures of creation for us. It remains for religion or philosophy to postulate answers to these questions. We are convinced that Christianity and the God of the Bible present the only adequate answers to such complex questions. Jastrow, although speaking from an agnostic perspective, notes this relationship between science and theology: "Now we would like to pursue that inquiry [concerning the origin of the universe] further back in time, but the barrier to further progress seems insurmountable. It is not a matter of another year, another decade of work, another measurement, or another theory; at this moment it seems as though science will never be able to raise the curtain on the mystery of creation. For the scientist who has lived by his faith in the power of reason, the story ends like a bad dream. He has scaled the mountains of ignorance; he is about to conquer the highest peak; as he pulls himself over the final rock, he is greeted by a band of theologians who have been sitting there for centuries."[19]

23

CHAPTER TWO

The Origin of the Universe

Throughout all of human history, we have tried to understand our universe and its origin. Man's art, literature, science, and religion have all reflected his desire to comprehend and make sense of the world around him. The ancient Egyptian sphinx reflects one religious idea about the heavens, typified in the zodiac. The space age highlights contemporary man's interest in exploring and explaining the heavens.

Many sophisticated religious descriptions and/or explanations of the universe developed quite early in recorded history, sometimes paralleling, sometimes diverging from the biblical *cosmology,* or understanding of the universe. The focus of this volume is on science and the universe. We will see how scientific investigation of the universe presents us with a cosmology absolutely consistent with the biblical cosmology. No ancient religious system other than the biblical one corresponds so closely to the scientific evidence uncovered in the last two centuries.

Ancient Religious Cosmologies

Many ancient religions attributed supernatural qualities and powers to natural forces and bodies. The Bible consistently differentiates between natural forces and bodies, the created order, and supernatural qualities and powers that belong only to the creator, God. Many ancient religions, for example, attributed the creation of the earth and its life to the sun, often referred to as the Supreme God. The ancient Egyptians named the sun god *Amun-Ra.* One of the most famous Egyptian literary pieces is a religious hymn of praise to *Aton* (another name for the sun god) as the creator of earthly life. Later Egyptian rulers also focused worship on the sun god as the Supreme God. Babylonian religion was the source of the ancient (and still living) system of astrology. In it the sun played a pivotal role as the source of earthly life.

Astrology is one ancient system used in an attempt to understand the heavens and to discover the future. The illustration is of the excavation of the ziggurat of the temple of Bel. Ziggurats were used for ancient astronomical and astrological purposes.

In general, ancient religions saw the sun as the supernatural source or sustainer of life. That view is not completely off the mark scientifically, since science has shown us the essential dependence on the sun of earthly life — for a variety of reasons, including our need for light, heat, etc. The ancient religions, however, erred in a significant way: they usually attributed supernatural power to the sun itself, seeing the sun as a god or the god over the earth. Scientists reject that hypothesis as "primitive" and "superstitious," postulating instead "natural law" or the "inherent order in the universe," or the "interdependency of the universe" as proper descriptions of the relationship between the sun and earth.

The Bible does not contradict the scientific evidence. It, too, rejects the idea of a supernatural sun god. It, too, sees law, order, and interdependency in the universe. But the Bible goes beyond science, and asserts the source of the law, order, and interdependency evident in the universe: an intelligent, benevolent, all-powerful, personal God outside the universe itself (that is, supernatural). The Bible recognizes the futility of locating the source of the universe within or as a part of the universe. At the same time, it goes beyond the inadequacy of the scientific model, which is unable to define the cause of the order it observes. Below we will discuss astrology as an example of ancient religions' attribution of supernaturalism to natural bodies and see its fatal shortcomings when compared to scientific observation.

Astrology

Modern astrology is defined as "The art of divining the fate or future of persons from the juxtaposition of the sun, moon, and planets. *Judicial astrology* foretells the destinies of individuals and nations, while *natural astrology* predicts changes of weather and the operation of the stars upon things."[1] Astrology presupposes, or takes for granted, that the heavenly bodies (stars, planets, moons, sun, comets, etc.) exert a causal influence on what happens on this earth. That presupposition is not limited to obvious and scientifically verifiable relationships, such as the pull of the moon's gravity on the earth's tides. It extends to all events and all personalities on the earth.

Today's astrology is based on complicated systems that have developed over thousands of years, combining the best of different systems from civilizations scattered around the globe. The ancient Egyptian tradition attributes the source of astrological knowledge to the god *Hermes Trismegistus,* or *Toth*, the one who delivered the messages of the gods. The Greeks and Romans had quite complicated astrological systems; parallel systems developed during the ancient historical periods of India and China. Some indications suggest that a primitive astrology existed in what we now know as Germany before that region's conversion to Christianity. During the Middle Ages the art of astrological prediction was spread by the Muslims through Spain and other Mediterranean countries to Catholics throughout Europe.

Above: Amun-Ra, the traditional Egyptian sun god. Pharaoh Akhenaten proclaimed the sun as the supreme god.
Below: An ancient fragment of Akhenaten's Hymn to Aton.

There are twelve signs of the Zodiac: the Northern (Commanding) signs are the first six, and the Southern (Obeying) signs are the second six. The twelve commonly accepted signs are Aries, Taurus, Gemini, Cancer, Leo, Virgo, Libra, Scorpio, Sagittarius, Capricorn, Aquarius, and Pisces. In addition, the planets (the sun is traditionally included here) and even some comets exert persuasive and causal power on things and events on this earth. A chart that displays the astrological influences in a person's life is called a *horoscope.*

Astronomer George O. Abell has summarized the ancient presupposition underlying ancient astrology:

"The Babylonians and Greeks...believed that human affairs were governed by capricious gods, whose embodiments were in the planets. Since each god, or planet, was a center of force, human lives must be programmed by the preset motions of the planets. What, then, can determine one's individual lot? Only the moment that he happens to enter the world and fall into step with the eternal and predestined movements of the heavens."[2]

Christian author Michael Van Buskirk provides a succinct summary of the presupposition underlying more contemporary astrology:

"One's future can be forecast, allegedly, because astrology asserts the unity of all things. This is the belief that the Whole (or all of the universe put together) is in some way the same as the Part (or the individual component or man), or that the Part is a smaller reflection of the Whole (macrocosmic/microcosmic model). This makes man a pawn in the cosmos with his life and actions pre-determined and unalterable."[3]

As an ancient religious cosmology, astrology had strong appeal. In a largely nonscientific society, astrological charting often was seen as an attempt to observe and classify order in the universe. Even more enticing was astrology's offer to reveal the mysterious future. Too, astrology's fatalism was comforting to those in dire straits (they had done nothing to deserve their bad fortune) and to those in opulence (it was their destiny to be rich). Astrology, however, fails the test of biblical cosmology and the test of scientific cosmology.

Astrology Fails Biblical Cosmology

Deuteronomy 18:9-12 explicitly names and condemns astrology. There was not to be found among God's people any who "useth divination, or an *observer of times,* or an enchanter, or a witch, or a charmer, or a consulter with familiar spirits, or a wizard, or a necromancer. For all that do these things are an abomination unto the LORD: and because

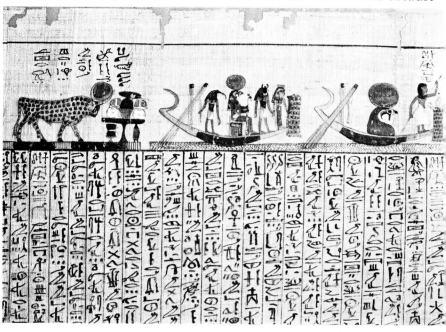

Right: Egyptian hieroglyphic picture of the sun god traversing the heavens in his boat. Below: A Babylonian relief of astrological significance.

of these abominations the LORD thy God doth drive them out from before thee."[4] That merely re-echos an earlier passage: "If there is found ...a man or a woman who...has gone and served other gods, and worshipped them, or *the sun, or the moon or any of the heavenly host* ...you shall bring out that man or that woman...and you shall stone them to death."[5] In the book of Daniel we find an interesting comparison between those dedicated to the true and living God and "all the magicians and *astrologers*" in Nebuchadnezzar's kingdom. Daniel and his friends were ten times better than all the magicians and astrologers in all wisdom and understanding.[6] The Old Testament prophet Isaiah consistently denied the power and authority of astrology, affirming instead the omnipotence of the biblical God who is the creator rather than part of the creation: "Thus says the LORD, your Redeemer, and the one who formed you from the womb, 'I, the LORD, am maker of all things, stretching out the heavens by Myself, and spreading out the earth all alone, causing the *omens* of boasters to fail, making fools out of *diviners*, causing wise men to draw back, and turning their knowledge into foolishness,"[7] and "Let now the *astrologers*, those who prophesy *by the stars*, those who predict *by the new moons*, stand up and save you from what will come upon you.

28

Right: Egyptian relief of Akhenaten and his wife, Nefretete.
Below: One of the features distinguishing Christianity from most ancient religions is that Christianity recognizes God as the creator of the heavens and the earth, while other religions worship the sun and/or other created things.

Behold, they have become like stubble, fire burns them; they cannot deliver themselves from the power of the flame; there will be no coal to warm by, nor a fire to sit before!...There is none to save you."[8]

The basic presupposition of astrology is completely contrary to the basic presupposition of the Bible, which distinguishes clearly between the creator and the creation, the supernatural and the natural.

Astrology Fails Scientific Cosmology

Astrology also is unable to meet the test of scientific investigation and observation. Many scientific critiques of astrology list dozens of verified scientific observations that are contradicted out of hand by the claims of astrology. Astronomer George O. Abell has traced the history of this scientific rejection of astrology:

"It was the growing recognition of the importance of empirical evidence that centuries ago led scientists to reject astrology, the polytheistic religion of antiquity. When the physical natures of the planets and the true laws that govern their motions became known, it simply stretched credibility too far to suppose that our destinies lie in the positions of the various planets, based on the times and places of our births, according to an arbitrary system of sky coordinates invented by man millennia ago."[9]

Almost all of the major world religious systems promote belief in some form of astrology. Christianity alone promotes the biblical view that the Creator is sovereign, man has free will and is not a victim of fate, and the stars and other heavenly bodies do not control people's destinies.

In our book, *Understanding the Occult*, we have outlined just nine of the serious problems astrology has with science.[10] In his booklet, Michael Van Buskirk mentions ten such problems.[11] Other writers, both Christian and secular, have presented similar catalogs of problems. Some of the most obvious are listed here.

1. Astrology is based on the theory that the earth is the center of this solar system (geocentricism). Scientific observation has shown conclusively that the sun is the center of this solar system (heliocentricism). "The consequence of this discovery is that all of the horoscopes ever cast are based on a false presupposition. How horoscopes can be reliable in any sense is a mystery...."[12]

2. Traditional astrology, from many different civilizations, recognizes seven "planets," including the sun and the moon. That not only mislabels the sun and moon, it also reveals early ignorance of the planets farthest from the sun and invisible to the naked eye. "According to the astrological theory...these three previously undiscovered planets should also have an influence upon behavior and must be considered to cast an exact horoscope. Since they usually are not considered, the astrological theory breaks down, for no accurate horoscope could be charted without considering all the planets and their supposed influence."[13]

3. Astrological charts are derived from select constellations, stars, and planets. The system for picking and choosing celestial influences is completely devoid of any scientific measuring or testing and is thus scientifically unreliable. "But if astrological influences are real, they have to arise from forces that emanate from some, but not all, celestial bodies, and that act on some, but not all, terrestrial things. Moreover, these forces cannot depend on the distance, size, mass, or other properties of their planets of origin; in other words, they lack the beauty, the symmetry, and the order of the laws and forces that we find everywhere in the real universe."[14]

4. Historical investigation exposes the random fickleness of astrological horoscopes. When birthdates and locations for a variety of unnamed persons are given to different astrologers who then "predict" their lives

An Indian concept of Creation (18th century). The god Vishnu stands on the turtle Avatare. The good gods have a tug of war with the bad gods (demons). From this turmoil comes creation.

by horoscopes, the results show the unreliability of astrology. "Forty birthdates were given to astrologers, twenty of well-known criminals and twenty of persons who had led long and peaceful lives. The astrologers were to separate the forty dates into the two proper classes on the basis of the horoscopes cast from the birthdates.... The astrologers invariably select a mixed bag of criminals and peaceful citizens in about the same proportion that a machine would pick randomly."[15]

5. Astrology is based on constellation measurements that are 2,000 years out of date and consequently unreliable. Although the positions of constellations in the earth's sky change over the years, astrology does not take that into account. "The early astronomers were not aware of precession and therefore failed to take it into account in their system.... due to precession, the constellations have shifted about 30 degrees in the last 2,000 years. This means that the constellation of Virgo is now in the sign of Libra, the constellation of Libra is now in the sign of Scorpio and so on. Thus, if a person is born on September 1, astrologers would call him a Virgo (the sign the sun is in at that date), but the sun is actually in the constellation Leo at that date. So there are two different zodiacs: one which slowly moves (the sidereal zodiac) and one which is stationary (the tropical zodiac). Which zodiac should be used?"[16]

6. Astrology is also logically untenable. It falls into the trap of being a victim of its own system. "They cannot have the objective authority necessary to explain our own world. If everything is predetermined in conjunction with the zodiac, then how can the astrologists get outside that fatalism to accurately observe it? What if the astrologists themselves are predetermined to explain everything by astrology? There is no way they can prove their system if they are pawns in that same system. By contrast, as Christians we can test our own world view because someone, Jesus Christ, has come from outside the 'system' to tell us, objectively, what our system is like."[17]

Those are just some of the main biblical and scientific objections to the ancient religious cosmology of astrology. It is completely incompatible

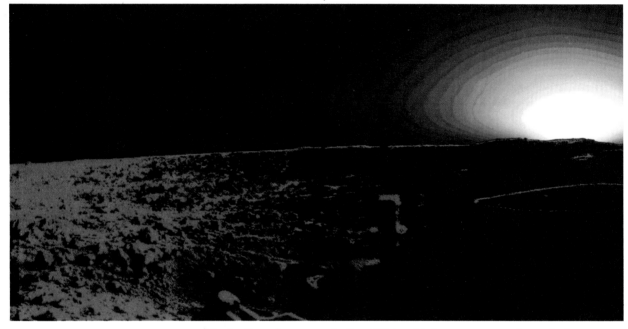

with both science and the Bible. It is representative of the many religious world views that cannot reconcile religious belief with scientific observation. As we shall see throughout this volume, only the Bible can reconcile religious belief with scientific observation.

Origins: Where Did the Universe Come From?

As we examine the origin of the universe throughout the pages of this volume, we will be discussing science and we will be discussing the Bible. Many times both will agree. That is not always the case, however. While we believe that all truth proceeds from God, who is truth, and that scientific truth can never contradict biblical truth, scientific suppositions and theories can contradict truth in numerous ways. The author of the Bible is the God of truth; scientists are not so infallible. Where science and the Bible absolutely conflict concerning origins, we will discuss those conflicts and show why science is, at that point, in error, and why the Bible is true. We do, though, want to reiterate that scientific truth is *not* in conflict with biblical truth. Christian author Bernard Ramm has observed:

"...To this extent science has opened up the secrets and meanings of Nature, the creation of God. To set theology against science is to oppose Creation to Revelation, and Nature to Redemption. Yet, it is

Above: Sunset on the planet Mars. Scientific observation over the centuries has removed the religious or astrological mystique from the other planets in our solar system, although they are still known by their mythological names.
Below: Human footprints on the surface of the moon underscore the increasing ability of man to explore his universe.

the uniform testimony of Scripture that the God and Christ of redemption are the God and Christ of creation."[18]

The domain of science is defined clearly in theory. In theory, it is the job of science to *observe* the natural world and seek to understand the natural world through that *observation*. It can often say "This happens," or "this is how such-and-such happens," but it is usually outside scientific jurisdiction to say "this is *why* such-and-such happens," or "this is the *value* of such-and-such event or process." *Why* and *value* are usually terms more properly associated with philosophy or religion than with science. In practice, scientists often overstep science's domain and attempt to deliver pronouncements on subjects with which science by definition is unable to deal. Biologist Jack Wood Sears notes:

"Approaching the matter from another way, science deals only with that which is timeless, repeatable at will, dependable, and universal. By this I mean that a scientist doing an experiment works only with those phenomena that are the same today as they were yesterday and as they will be tomorrow. He cannot deal with the unique, the thing that happens only once, for science relies for verification not upon one experiment but on repeated experiments. A scientist in the laboratory does his experiment today and expects to be able to do it again tomorrow with the same results. For science deals with phenomena that are not only timeless but also repeatable at will. Should a scientist perform an experiment today and then in attempting to repeat the experiment get different results, he would not publish this as a new discovery. Rather he would go back over his two experiments to try to determine what caused the difference in results. You see the scientist believes in the dependability of nature, and of the natural laws and so doubts any experimental results that cannot be proved through repetition."[19]

Possible Origins of the Universe

Although one at first might think that there are dozens of possible origins of the universe, there are actually only three. Once we have dispensed with the idea that the universe doesn't exist at all but is some sort of illusion, we are faced with three basic alternatives for its origin. No matter which of the hundreds of theories of origins one picks, any theory will fit into one of three possible origins. It does not take great scientific knowledge to figure out those three alternatives: it takes only logic and common sense. The three alternatives are:

1. The universe is not eternal but just popped into existence with no pre-existent cause;

2. The universe is itself eternal, although it may have changed form at various times; or

3. The universe is not eternal but came into existence at a point in time, and was caused by something or someone other than itself.

As a matter of fact, possibilities one and three are variations of the same idea and so we could narrow the possibilities to two: the universe is either eternal or not eternal. We shall first deal with the idea that the universe is an illusion, and then we will be concerned primarily with ideas two and three, since science and the Bible both agree that a thing

An artist's rendition of the "big bang," said by many scientists to mark the creation of the universe.

cannot cause itself or have a finite (not eternal) existence without any cause at all.

Is the universe an illusion? Most people would laugh at the idea that the universe is an illusion, but some philosophers and religious thinkers have argued for the idea that the universe, or all of existence as we know it, is illusory or transitory. Some assert that the world we see around us and in which we live is not a real world after all, but is either a shadow or dream or hallucination or thought of the eternal and all-pervading god. Such thinkers often say that talk about the origin of the universe is silly since the universe doesn't really exist anyway.

Rather than belaboring our response, we can answer such a thinker simply. Does he believe *anything* exists? If he does, then what does he believe really exists (God, himself, etc.)? As soon as he tells us what he believes that has real existence, then we ask him, "Where did that real thing come from? What is its origin?" We have now faced him with the same alternatives we shall explore here: this real thing was created spontaneously with no cause; it is eternal; or it was created by something or someone outside itself. If anyone actually asserts that he believes *nothing* exists, then we don't have to talk to him, because he and we, along with everything else, have no existence. Nobody is talking to nobody about nothing.

34

Did the universe cause itself? Returning to our three viable options for the origin of the universe, we see that option one can be dealt with easily because it postulates the unscientific and unbiblical hypothesis that something (the universe) can come from nothing (self-caused). Christian philosopher Richard Purtill comments on the obvious problems with alternative one:

"The real choice, of course, is between the second and third alternatives, for hardly anyone takes the first alternative seriously. Because it will be useful later, we will briefly see why the first alternative is so implausible. One thing we could say about the possibility of the universe simply coming into existence from nothing is to declare that nothing comes

The second law of thermodynamics, or entropy, is observable all around in our universe. The fact is that the universe and each of its components tend toward disorder, randomness, corruption, and/or death.

from nothing... but suppose that someone denies the inconceivability of something from nothing. What can we say to him? We can, of course, challenge him to cite an instance of something coming from nothing, and if he does so he may reveal a misunderstanding of what he is denying. He may, for example, cite the theory of continuous creation held by some scientific cosmologists. But this theory does not claim that matter comes into existence from nothing, but says that in certain areas of space matter is formed from energy, rather as drops of dew condense from water vapor. Even if this theory were true it would no more contradict the principle that nothing comes from nothing than the creation of dewdrops from water vapor.

"Suppose, however, that the denial did not rest on a misunderstanding and the objector seriously maintained that things can just pop into existence for no reason at all. We could point out that if this happened at the beginning of the universe there would be no reason why it should not happen now. We could point out that no one would take seriously the idea that anything—a baseball, a planet, even a snowflake—had simply popped into existence from nothing. The impossibility of this sort of thing is a basic assumption of any coherent thinking about the universe. For if any explanation of the existence of any particular thing may be just it popped into existence for no reason, and if the ultimate explanation of everything is just that, then all explanation is undermined. So to hold the pop theory of the origin of the universe is to give up any hope of rationality or understandability in the universe. If someone claims to hold this view then he cannot be reached by rational argument, for he has abandoned rationality. But if someone abandons rationality he can have no reason for holding any view, and no reason for action except momentary passion or appetite. He has, in effect, stepped out of the human race down to the animal level. This is a solution of sorts to some problems, but then so is suicide."[20]

So, then, our actual choices concerning the origin of the universe are

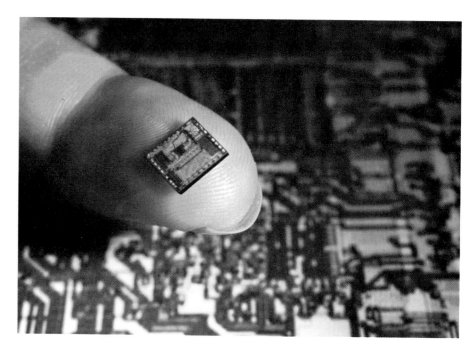

Right: Just as a sophisticated computer chip must be carefully designed and "programmed," so our sophisticated universe testifies that it has been carefully designed and programmed. Below: Science-fiction writer Isaac Asimov acknowledges the complexity of the universe in his books, but fails to associate such complexity with a designer, or God.

that it is either *eternal*, or that it had a *beginning*.

Is the universe eternal? Most people who declare that the universe is eternal do not actually believe that the universe had no beginning. Usually they say it is "eternal" because they cannot imagine a time when the universe was not in existence. This universe is the only dimension with which they are familiar and it seems impossible to think of a time when what is, wasn't. Usually such people are confusing the idea that this universe is the only dimension in all of existence. Those who because of arbitrary thought patterns are unable to conceive of anything outside this universe are like the prejudiced inhabitants of the science-fiction world of Flatland.

Edwin A. Abbott, in his now-classic *Flatland,* "wrote" the journal of a two-dimensional square who miraculously discovered and traveled in the three-dimensional world, returned to his own dimension, and was imprisoned by the prejudiced and narrow-minded inhabitants of his two-dimensional world for daring to tell his countrymen that there existed a dimension beyond their own. The importance of recognizing the possibility of existence outside our own narrow world is summarized by the square from Flatland, who lamented at the end of his journal:

"Prometheus up in Spaceland was bound for bringing down fire for mortals, but I—poor Flatland Prometheus—lie here in prison for bringing down nothing to my countrymen. Yet I exist in the hope that these memoirs, in some manner, I know not how, may find their way to the minds of humanity in Some Dimension, and may stir up a race of rebels who shall refuse to be confined to limited Dimensionality."[21] Narrowmindedness is insufficient justification for postulating an eternal universe.

What, then, of those who understand the illogic of an eternal universe and still postulate one? Such people are usually of one of two persuasions: they have a religious presupposition that assumes an

The complexity of the universe is reflected in the intricate planetary relationships in our own solar system. The picture is of the earth's horizon just after sunset, with Venus clearly visible.

eternal universe, or, they mistakenly think that scientific evidence supports an eternal universe theory. Those who accept an eternal universe on religious grounds must be answered on other than scientific ground, and we are precluded by space limitations from dealing with them here. We recommend our *Understanding Non-Christian Religions* for further information regarding that kind of objection.[22]

Those who accept an eternal universe because of a misunderstanding of scientific evidence show ignorance of the two most fundamental laws of physics: the law of conservation of energy ("The sum total of mass and energy in this universe is neither created nor destroyed") and the law of entropy ("Every process in the universe tends toward nonrecoverable energy loss"). Dr. Henry Morris describes these two laws and their relevance to the question of the origin of the universe:

"The basic principle of all physical science is that of the conservation and deterioration of energy. The law of energy conservation states that in any transformation of energy in a closed system from one sort into another, the total amount of energy remains unchanged. A similar law is the law of mass conservation, which states that although matter may be changed in size, state, form, etc., the total mass cannot be changed. In other words, these laws teach that no creation or destruction of matter or energy is now being accomplished anywhere in the physical universe*.... This law of mass and energy conservation is also known as the first law of thermodynamics, and is almost without controversy the most important and basic law of all physical science....

"The second law of thermodynamics, of almost as great significance, enunciates the corollary law of energy deterioration. In any energy transfer or change, although the total amount of energy remains unchanged, the amount of usefulness and availability that the energy possesses is always decreased. This principle is also called the law of entropy increase, entropy being a sort of mathematical abstraction which is actually a measure of the nonavailability of the energy of a

Stars are massed in a variety of configurations, including that above. The stars in a galaxy rotate with varying velocities.

system.... The same principle applies to all the stars of the universe, so that the physical universe is, beyond question, growing old, wearing out and running down.

"But this law certainly testifies equally to the necessary truth that the universe had a definite beginning. If it is growing old, it must once have been young; if it is wearing out, it must once have been new; if it is running down, it must first have been 'wound up.'"[23]

So we see that scientific evidence points to the two facts that matter is neither created nor destroyed and that every process in the universe tends toward a loss of available energy. The phenomena that testify to these two laws is testimony to the fact that the universe is not eternal but had a beginning.

The universe had a beginning. We have made several biblically and scientifically important observations in this chapter. We have asserted that the biblical and scientific cosmologies have more in common with each other and with truth than either has with any other religious or nonreligious cosmology. We have seen that it is illogical to believe that

---

*Mass and energy are not necessarily independently constant, but the sum total of mass and energy together is constant.

the universe is illusory. We then saw that it does not make sense scientifically or logically to say that the universe caused itself. We have just discussed the scientific reasoning behind a rejection of the eternal universe theory. We are left finally with the alternative that makes scientific and biblical sense: the universe was created (had an origin), and was created by something or someone outside itself. The remainder of this book will deal with this observation.

Christian scholar E. M. Blaiklock delineated the challenge to accept a created universe as follows:

"You can doggedly believe, if you will, that the vision of order and interlocking purpose which we see all around us is a mere fortuitous congregation of atoms, such as Democritus pictured twenty-three centuries ago, plunging through some inconceivable void. Or you can

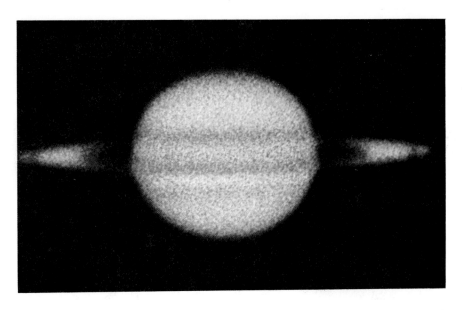

Right: The planet Uranus, which rotates on its axis in the opposite direction of that of the earth. Below: A solar eclipse.

believe that a Mind has ordered it all. Lecomte de Nouy, the French physicist, has expressed in figures, which an eminent mathematician assures me are sound, the chances loaded against the fortuitous formation of one protein molecule. They are beyond imagination. The figures, too, may be related to both space and time. Such an event would require a volume of matter fantastically larger than the whole mass of the Einsteinian universe, with a radius, in fact, of 10^{82} light years, or, if the molecule envisaged is to be formed within that mass, it would require statistically 10^{243} billions of years for the event. The figures baffle comprehension.

"You may confidently tell me that any such chance event could happen before lunch, but I call to your remembrance that we speak of one protein molecule. How many millions compose my little finger, I do not know. If you will, you can doggedly believe that an unimaginably complex array of interlocking juxtapositions of atoms have produced the universe, the human person, those agitations within us which we call faith, hope, love, poetry, and beauty...but it seems to me that to accept such a basis on which to build your life and peace—and that application assuredly follows—you need a sturdier faith than mine when I chose to believe that a great Intelligence has ordered it all. Such a conclusion can certainly not be laughed away."[24]

The Universe: A Grand Design

Left: The earth photographed from Apollo XI.
Right: This complicated topographical pattern highlights the complexity of the earth's composition.

We ended our last chapter with the reasonable conclusion that the universe really exists, it is not eternal, and it did not create itself. In this chapter we will observe the design apparent in the universe which tells us something about the creator of the universe. Because of the grand, intelligent, ordered, and purposeful design we see imprinted in the universe and its parts, we can extrapolate the existence of a creator who is infinite, intelligent, and purposeful.

Remember, science *observes*, it does not answer *why* questions, and so science can never really *prove* the existence of God. If we assume that there is a God, however, and that He did create the universe, and that He is the infinite, intelligent, powerful, and benevolent God the Bible says He is, then He would leave just such "traces" or "evidences" in His world as we find in our universe. We could almost say that the universe bears the "signature" of God. Christian scientist Henry M. Morris says: "The obvious conclusion is that complex, ordered structures of any kind (and the world is full of them) simply could never have happened by chance. Disorder never spontaneously turns into order. Organization requires an organizer. The infinite array of complex effects seen in the universe must have been produced by an adequate cause. An adequate Cause is God, the Creator, and nothing less!"[1]

Right: An ancient patterned depiction of the creation and the Garden of Eden. While such pictures are numerous, they are meant to typify the Genesis story, not to picture it scientifically.

Below: A classic interpretation of the expulsion of Adam and Eve from Paradise after their sin.

What About the Disorder in the Universe?

Preliminary to our review of order in the universe, we need to address the question of the disorder we also see in the universe. If order implies a creator, does disorder imply a "non-creator," or that, perhaps, "chance" created some things while God created others?

Not at all. When the vast reaches of the universe display such sophisticated intelligent design as scientists can observe today, the proportionately smaller degree of disorder serves as testimony to an *interruption* or *corruption* of the grand design of the universe. That is exactly what the Bible declares. God is the Creator of the universe, but he gave mankind the highest honor possible in the created order. The Bible describes the Lord's glory and the dignity with which he endowed mankind:

"When I consider Thy heavens, the work of Thy fingers, the moon and the stars, which Thou hast ordained; what is man, that Thou dost take thought of him? And the son of man, that Thou dost care for him? Yet Thou hast made him a little lower than God, and dost crown him with glory and majesty! Thou dost make him to rule over the works of Thy hands; Thou hast put all things under his feet."[2]

It is no wonder, then, that when mankind deliberately broke its relationship with God, the entire creation felt and continues to feel the effects of that corruption. This is what the Bible says. From the time that Adam and Eve sinned and were banished from God's presence, the effects of corruption have manifested themselves throughout the creation. The apostle Paul, in his letter to the Romans, said:

"For the anxious longing of the creation waits eagerly for the revealing of the sons of God. For the creation was subject to futility, not of its own will, but because of Him who subjected it, in hope that the creation itself also will be set free from its slavery to corruption into the freedom of the glory of the children of God. For we know that the whole creation groans and suffers the pains of childbirth together until now."[3]

So, then, the presence of corruption or disorder in the universe does not

One of the methods used to determine the age of the remains of living things is Carbon-14 dating. Measuring the amount of Carbon-14 left in the organism can date the remains accurately only if the basic assumption of uniformitarianism is accepted.

negate the testimony of the overall design and order in the universe to the existence of an intelligent and all-powerful creator.*

Who Is the Creator?

We can turn to the Bible for a clear description of the creator of the universe, and of the manner in which He created everything. The Bible is not primarily a science text, but rather the revelation of God to mankind. It does not, however, err scientifically in any of its statements. In addition, the creation of the universe is one of the mighty acts of God and so is described and alluded to in several places in Scripture. The apostle Paul described the creator as "the God who made the world and all things in it, since He is Lord of heaven and earth, does not dwell in temples made with hands; neither is He served by human hands, as though He needed anything, since He Himself gives all life and breath and all things."[4] This is how the creator has described Himself: "I, the Lord, am the maker of all things, stretching out the heavens by Myself, and spreading out the earth all alone."[5]

---

*We are here distinguishing between destructive corruption and beneficial "disordering" processes, such as common diffusion, etc.

In graphic symbolism, God described His creative acts to Job, challenging him to rise to the grandeur of the creator of the universe:

"Where were you when I laid the foundation of the earth! Tell Me, if you have understanding, who set its measurements, since you know? Or who stretched the line on it? On what were its bases sunk? Or who laid its cornerstone, when the morning stars sang together, and all the sons of God shouted for joy? Or who enclosed the sea with doors, when, bursting forth, it went out from the womb; when I made a cloud its garment, and thick darkness its swaddling band, and I placed boundaries on it, and I set a bolt and doors, and I said, 'Thus far you shall come, but no farther; and here shall your proud waves stop'?"

Above: Radioactive dating methods calculate the age of this rock formation in Greenland at 3800 million years old. This dating method also assumes uniformitarianism.
Below: Basalt-like igneous rock possesses a beautifully iridescent microscopic structure.

The artistic figures of speech recorded here in Job give an almost visionary picture of the mighty power necessary to create and harness the universe.

Genesis 1 makes specific statements about the original creation of the universe. In later chapters we will discuss science and biblical account of human creation. Here we will concern ourselves with the major claims of Genesis 1 concerning the origin of the universe.

Dating and the Bible

There are Christian scholars who believe that the Bible sets very definite limits on the age of the universe, the earth, and mankind. There are also many non-Christian scholars who dismiss any biblical notion of creation because they believe the Bible specifically limits the age of the universe; the earth, and/or mankind. Before we deal specifically with Genesis 1, we need to explain our own understanding of the Bible's dating of origins.

In the opinion of the author of the American version of this *Family Handbook of Christian Knowledge,* the age of the universe, the earth, and mankind is not specifically limited or determined by Scripture. We do not have space here to bring up all of the theological, biblical, and scientific reasons that has led him, and many other Christian and non-Christian scholars, to that conclusion. (See the recommended reading list at the end of this volume or our *Reasons Skeptics Should Consider Christianity* and *Answers to Tough Questions* for more information on this question.) We believe that every word of the autographs (originals) of Scripture are without error in any way, and that valid and reasonable interpretations of relevant Scripture passages can argue either for a very ancient creation or a more recent one. We respect serious Bible scholars on both sides of the argument, as long as those scholars hold to reasonable explanations for their convictions, and as long as their convictions are based on belief in the inerrancy of Scripture. In a survey discussion such as this, however, the author does not see any compelling

Right: The Sinai desert rock formation is testimony to the mighty forces which mold the earth's surface.
Below: The mineral torbernite is igneous rock.

reason to assert dogmatically one position or the other. The important thing is that neither biblical interpretation denies the *evidence* (not necessarily the *assumptions*) of science. Christian author James Jauncey presents a reasonable summary:

"Although there has been some conflict between science and religion for centuries, the problem did not come out into clear relief until the end of the eighteenth century and the beginning of the nineteenth. That was the time when the new geological discoveries were being made. It soon became possible that instead of an earth 6000 years old, as it had been generally believed, it could have gone back millions of years. This seemed to many people a direct challenge to the Biblical message.

"As we see it now, this point of conflict was rather unnecessary. Most of it was due to the rather unfortunate researches of an Irish archbishop named Ussher in the seventeenth century. Apparently he was also an amateur mathematician. As the result of his calculations, he concluded that creation occurred in 4004 B.C. Since he was an archbishop, most Christian people assumed he was correct. The date soon appeared in the margins of Bible and still exists in many Bibles today.

"The Bible makes no such stipulation. It simply says that in the beginning God created the heavens and the earth. According to this it

Problems in the accuracy of radiometric dating assumptions are illustrated by the attempt to verify it by testing rocks whose date of composition is known. Igneous rock formed after the eruption of the Hawaiian volcano Kilauea 200 years ago was dated radiometrically at 22 million years old.

could just as easily have been millions of years ago as just a few thousand years ago. You can see that the problem was science versus Ussher rather than science versus the Bible. The point no longer raises serious difficulty."

Creation Reflects God's Design

For the rest of the chapter, we will examine the first creative claims of Genesis 1 concerning the origin of the universe. To do that will give us an outline of the biblical creation of cosmology and its harmony with the scientific creation cosmology. There is no final conflict between scientific evidence and the biblical record. But there is often conflict between scientific prejudice and the biblical record, and/or between scientific evidence and faulty interpretation of the biblical record.

"In the beginning God created the heavens and the earth. And the earth was formless and void, and darkness was over the surface of the deep; and the Spirit of God was moving over the surface of the waters. Then God said, 'Let there be light'; and there was light. And God saw that the light was good; and God separated the light from the darkness. And God called the light day, and the darkness He called night...Then God said, 'Let there be an expanse in the midst of the waters, and let it separate the waters from the waters.' And God made the expanse, and separated the waters which were below the expanse from the waters which were above the expanse; and it was so...Then God said, 'Let the waters below the heavens be gathered into one place. And let the dry land appear' and it was so" (Genesis 1:1-9).

That statement of God's order of creation on the earth, offering a kind of harmony between the biblical account and scientific evidence, is a testimony to the creative power of God. (The origin of life will be discussed in the next chapter.)

God Created the Physical Universe

Genesis 1 disallows the view that claims that the universe is eternal. The heavens and the earth (the universe) are not eternal. They "began to be,"

Right: One of the recently formed islands of the Vestmann group south of Iceland. These islands are formed by submarine volcanic eruption.
Below: Nobel Prize winner Dr. W. Libby devised the Carbon-14 dating method.

or were created. If one looks at one postulate of science ("matter can neither be created nor destroyed"[8]), one could assume falsely that the universe is eternal. However, that postulate must be understood with its requisite presupposition and in conjunction with another fundamental postulate of science. The presupposition to the first postulate is that within this system, the universe, matter can neither be created nor destroyed. It says nothing about the origin of the matter which now exists, and does not deny that the matter which now exists did come into being at some time. The second postulate of science which correlates to this first one is that of *entropy*, or the scientific observation that every process in the universe results in a product with less usable energy than was available before the process. In other words, everything is slowing down, cooling off, losing its dynamic potential. If the matter we have now cannot be created or destroyed, and if all matter is losing its available energy, then Genesis 1:1's claim that the heavens and the earth (the universe) were created is substantiated by scientific observation.

Christian scientist Peter W. Stoner comments on the correlation between Genesis 1:1 and scientific evidence:

"*All Stars Had a Beginning.* The radiation of our sun is apparently produced by the loss of about 4,200,000 tons of mass a second. Only about 1/200th part of this is recovered. This means that the sun is running down. The same can be said for all of the other stars. If the stars are all running down, they must have had a beginning. They could not have always existed, for if four million tons of mass are added to the sun each second for an infinite period of past time you would have an infinite mass and our sun would have started by filling all space. The same can be said for each of the 100 billion stars in each of the trillions of galaxies. This is impossible. Therefore, every star had a beginning.

"Genesis 1:1 does not state a time when the universe was created. As far as scriptural evidence is concerned it does not matter whether everything started five or six billion years ago, ten billion years ago, one hundred billion years ago, or any other assigned time....

The Barringer crater in Arizona (1250 meters wide by 175 meters deep) was formed from the impact of a large meteor.

A very old magnetic compass. The earth's magnetic field may give a clue to the age of the earth.

"This evidence is so strong that many astronomers are freely talking about the day of creation. They are even forming theories as to how the universe was created. Some speculation seems to hinge about the concept that the universe was created from a tremendous amount of energy, probably in the form of light. One of these theories would have this energy change to matter in a remarkably short time, requiring no longer than one-half hour.

"Thus Genesis 1:1 is no longer contradictory to science, but completely agrees with both the best facts and theories of science today."[9]

Genesis 1 goes on to state that the earth was without form, and void. While scientific theory has gone back and forth with myriad ideas about the formation of the solar system, the theories that appear to fit the evidence best, and appear to be most reasonable, are also those theories in harmony with this statement in Genesis. One popular theory for a long time was the Nebular Hypothesis, which supposed that a gaseous body in space rotated slowly. As it cooled, it rotated more and more quickly, reducing its area and increasing its mass, until it was able to form separate rotating bodies (the planets in our solar system).

The currently popular theory is that star systems or planetary systems are descendants or developments of dark (or black) nebulas. This is in harmony with Genesis 1:2. Having our earth produced from a dark nebula would also account for the evidence that the earth was once much hotter than it is now, and is continually cooling. For example, igneous rock is rock that was once molten (lava) and then cooled to a solid form.

The second half of Genesis 1:2 states, literally, that the Spirit of God

Careful research in population statistics seems to indicate that, if man has really been on earth for more than one million years, the earth's population would actually be many times larger than it is.

was moving, "brooded," over the waters, much as a bird "broods" over its eggs. If all life originated with the creative power of God, then one should find the biblical record attesting to the presence of God acting with the elements from which life was created. This is what we find here. In addition, we find that the Spirit of God was participating in a dynamic nurturing of the elements from which life was created. One immediately pictures the common scientific scenario of a vast ocean of elements, constantly in motion, and "nurtured" in a temperature and solution most conducive to the formation of the most primitive life forms.

Genesis 1:3 even distinguishes the kind and source of light that illuminated the young earth. Rather than committing a common early religious mistake of placing the source of earthly light in or around the earth, the Scripture notes that the light came a distance from the earth, illuminating one part of the earth at a time, allowing for the distinguishing of day from night. That is just what happens when light comes from the sun to the earth, illuminating half of the earth at one time.

Science postulates from contemporary observation that as the young earth aged and cooled, water vapor condensed and for the first time

Above: The legs of the lunar lander were designed to keep the structure balanced on top of the lunar dust, which was not nearly as deep as one would expect if the moon had been accumulating the dust over millions of years. Below: If the earth is actually millions of years old, it is remarkable that oil and gas deposits have not completely dissipated into surrounding rock through seepage.

remained in its liquid form on the surface of the young planet. Genesis 1:6-8 is in complete harmony with this scientific model and even follows the model a step further in verse 9 by noting that dry land was the next to appear, scientifically explained by the uneven cooling and contraction of the earth's surface.

Peter W. Stoner summarized his ideas concerning the scientific veracity of Genesis 1 in this way:

"We have shown that by very recent developments of science Genesis 1 agrees perfectly with all of the sciences concerned. There does not appear to be a contradiction of any magnitude still remaining. There is, however, this extremely strong argument, or proof, for the Bible's truth."[10]

The grand design of the universe is mirrored in the creation of the earth. We have seen from our brief survey of the origin section of Genesis 1 and from our comparison of that section with today's science, that an intelligent, benevolent, all-powerful creator, outside this universe, is the author of both the universe and the Bible.

The scientist who postulates chance as responsible for the origin of the universe is negating any idea of real order, design, predictability, or pattern in the universe. The best that such a person can postulate is a random and meaningless universe that gives a false *illusion* of order, design, predictability, and pattern. And yet that same scientist presupposes and relies on the existence of logic and order in almost everything he does or thinks. Science is based on the premise that there is order in the universe and that the order in the universe can be observed, measured, and used to understand the world in which we live. If there were no order in the universe, there could be no science.

If, however, an intelligent designer, God, created the universe with inherent design and order, then the scientist's task is *not* futile; we can learn a lot from science about our fascinating world.

Many unsophisticated religious
world views exist, including the
once-popular idea of the three-
storied universe— a flat earth,
floating on water, surrounded
by firmament. However, the Bible,
while using common figures of
speech, does not contradict
scientific observation in
any way.

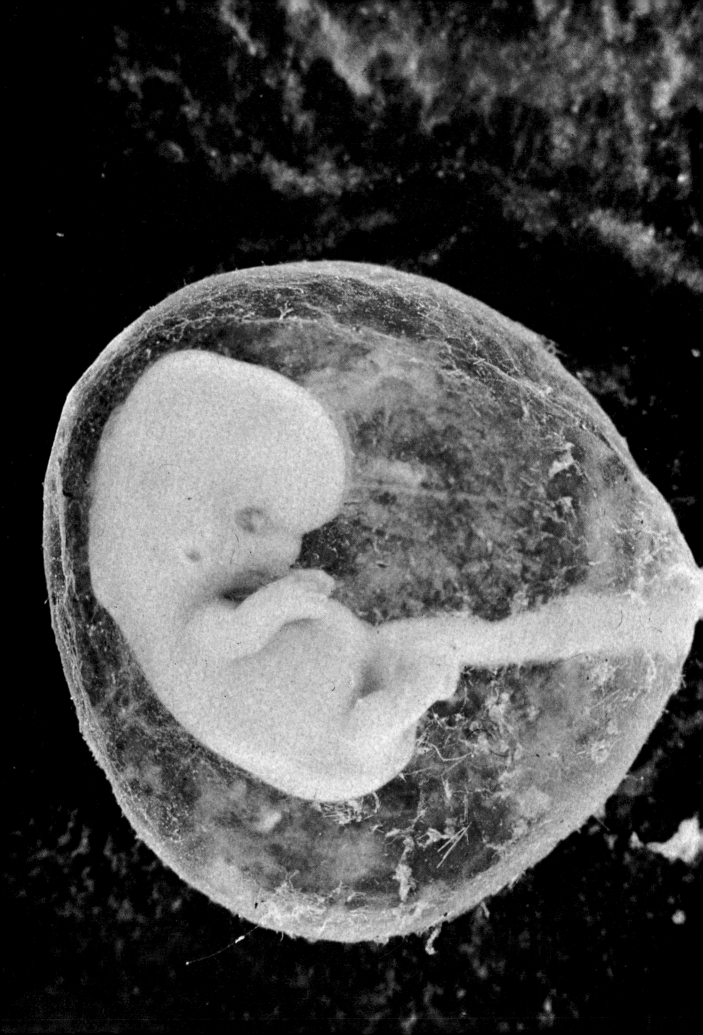

CHAPTER FOUR

The Origin of Life

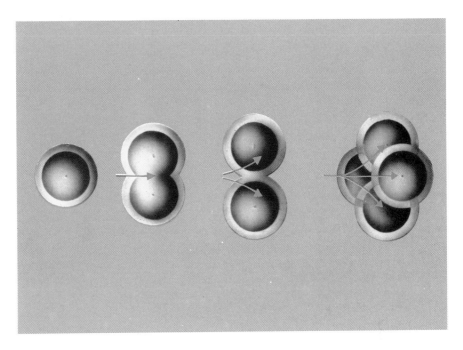

The wonders of new life! The beginning of new human life is breathtakingly beautiful. After the egg is fertilized by the sperm, everything that the new person will become develops from that one initial cell. Just twenty-one days after fertilization, the embryo has the basic form of a human being. Two months after fertilization the face appears; arms and legs, with their finger and toe buds, are clearly discernible. Three months after fertilization, at twelve weeks, tiny fingernails and genitalia are distinct.

At the end of an average nine months' gestation, the new little person is born, a living, breathing, growing, and, most uniquely, a thinking individual. New life, especially human life, is a miracle. One must almost start with an antisupernatural bias to assume that the fascinating intricacy of reproduction is the result of unconscious chance.

Let's look again at a fertilized human egg, a "person under construction." This activated zygote has the potential to be a complex living mechanism which, even at birth, will be several thousand million times heavier than the original zygote. How can one small living cell metamorphose so radically, and yet with overwhelmingly ordered and designed components? How do the multiplying cells know to differentiate, to grow, to cluster, to divide, to make a human being? How does one cell know to be a particular part of a bone, and another

53

cell know to be a particular part of an organ? Scientists can describe cells. They can point to the components within cells that contain the genetic and reproductive information utilized by the cell. But scientists can't answer the *why* of life. Why did life develop? Why did life differentiate? Why do various life forms resemble each other? Why are there distinctions among life forms? Those who give the answer "evolution" are not *explaining*, they are only *describing* one possible chain of events. They are not answering *why*. In the final analysis, life remains a mystery to the scientist.

Cellular Life

When we take a closer look at a cell, we find an incredibly complex structure with various internal "organs" that work together so that the

Michelangelo's concept of the creation of man by God. The painting adorns part of the ceiling of the Sistine Chapel in the Vatican at Rome.

cell will function as it should. The cell absorbs food, secretes waste products (and thus has a simple metabolism) and even can produce by division. In the center of the cell is the nucleus, which contains at least part of the information the cell needs to function properly. The nucleus contains the chromosomes, long strands whose most important component is DNA (deoxyribonucleic acid). DNA is the actual genetic material which determines hereditary characteristics. A DNA molecule looks schematically somewhat like a twisted ladder. When the cell divides, the "ladder" splits lengthwise down the center and each half forms a separate and new chain.

Chromosomes consist of molecules; each molecule consists of a number of atoms. Most living cells contain molecules that consist of combinations of six elements: carbon, hydrogen, oxygen, nitrogen, phosphorus, and sulphur. The amazing complexity, diversity, and order we see in the living world around us has these six basic elements as its building blocks.

The Bible does not contradict this scientific observation, as we see in Genesis 2:7 ("the LORD God formed man of *dust* from the ground") and Genesis 3:19 ("...till you return to the ground, because from it you

Plant life was created by God on the third day, according to Genesis.

were taken; for you are dust, and to dust you shall return").

But living organisms are more than just a few chemical elements arranged in particular patterns. A corpse, for example, still consists of the same chromosomes, the same molecules, the same atoms, the same elements, as a living person. But the corpse is not living. At death the corpse immediately begins disintegration, corruption. The heart no longer beats, the eyes no longer see, the brain no longer functions. Life is gone. Scientists can observe differences between living and non-living things. They can observe characteristics of dying things. But they cannot *explain* what life is.

Human life is different from other forms of life, no matter how much modern materialists may insist that a human being is no more than a sophisticated machine. Only humans have self-cognizance, the ability to recognize themselves and their relationship to the rest of reality. That capacity is part of what the Bible means when it says we are made in God's *image:*

"Then God said, 'Let Us make man in Our image, according to Our likeness; and let them rule over the fish of the sea and over the birds of the sky and over the cattle and over all the earth, and over every creeping thing that creeps on the earth.' And God created man in His own image, in the image of God He created him, male and female He created them."[1]

Christian writer Harry Rimmer describes the difference between human and other life, and science's inability to account for that difference, in this way:

"Again, in the science of embryology, there is no living authority who can say whence the quickening life comes that brings conscious existence into the cell mass that is called the fetus. The major mystery in this complicated science is the coming of that life which is called soul, or spirit, and which animates the mass of biological substance with intelligent entity, comprehension, and the functions of will."[2]

It is important to note the significant difference between humans and any other life form. Not only are humans very different from plants, but humans are also very different from animals. Only humans, according to the Bible, are made "in God's image." Only we humans possess the will and self-consciousness that distinguishes us so sharply from even the most "advanced" and intelligent animals. Anatomist Kingsley Mortimer discusses that difference:

"To the scientist, man is an animal, graciously self-designated as *homo sapiens.* I have no wish, and this is not the place, to discuss whether man is an animal or not. If he is, at least he is still the only one discussing what kind of animal he is. Few, however, would deny that man, animal or not, has features without parallel in any other member of that kingdom. We are quite familiar with the physical evidence that marks out *homo sapiens*—the erect posture, the grasping thumb, the cerebral hemispheres. These are all acceptable criteria and have been with us for a long time. Few men take pride in them, but rather take them for granted. They are standard equipment.

"What puts man in the luxury class among all forms of life is his unique capacity for thought, and his possession of free will. He can do as he

Genesis states that God created light on the first day, but caused light to shine on the earth from the sun and (reflectively) the moon on the fourth day. Lightning is one example of a natural light source independent of the sun.

likes; he can go it alone. By his own choice, he can know the mystery of loneliness and solitary rebellion. Indeed, the very capacity to be rebellious or miserable is probably the property of man alone. For who ever hears of a miserable rose or a rebellious kangaroo?

"More than any other creature, man looks outside himself more than he cares to look within. It is easier; it is comforting; it is what other people do. It is common today to confuse environment with satisfaction, to believe that one necessarily conditions and controls the other. This is part of the overreach (not the outreach) of the Darwinian hypothesis."[3]

In this chapter we will explore the scientific and biblical scenarios for the origin of life. How did life begin on earth? What kind of life was it? What was requisite for life to begin? How do scientific speculations on the origin of life compare to the biblical account of the origin of life?

The Biblical Account of the Origin of Life

According to Genesis, life was created by God on the third "day" of creation. (It is not necessary for our discussion here to determine the length of the creative days of Genesis. We refer interested readers to the recommended reading for information on that subject.) As we saw in chapter three, God first created the heavens and the earth, dark and formless. He created light, and He brought light to the earth on a day/ night schedule. As the earth cooled, some of the water vapor in which

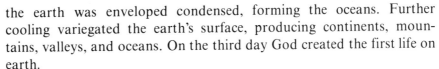

the earth was enveloped condensed, forming the oceans. Further cooling variegated the earth's surface, producing continents, mountains, valleys, and oceans. On the third day God created the first life on earth.

"Then God said, 'Let the earth sprout vegetation, plants yielding seed, and fruit trees bearing after their kind, with seed in them, on the earth'; and it was so. And the earth brought forth vegetation, plants yielding seed after their kind, and trees bearing fruit, with seed in them, after their kind."[4]

There are several points to note here to which we will return later. First, even though Genesis records that light first shone from the sun on the fourth day, after the creation of plant life, there was already light by which photosynthesis could take place (Genesis 1:3-5). Second, it is important to note that the plants were created with reproductive capability from the beginning. Third, we note that the plants were to reproduce only after their own kind. That becomes especially important in chapter five, where we discuss the theory of macroevolution, or the development of one life form from a different life form.

Before God created plant life, he created the environment that was capable of supporting that life. He created cycles of light and darkness, water, and atmosphere. Although the Bible clearly states that God *created* the first plant life, most scientists dissent sharply. Starting with

57

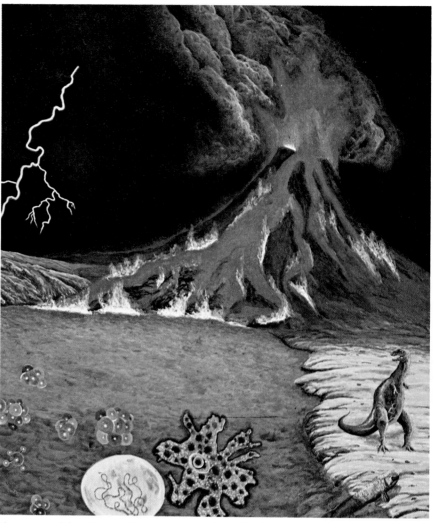

An artistic representation of the general theory of evolution. Life emerges spontaneously from the primeval "soup" and evolves into increasingly complex forms.

the same friendly environment as described above, scientists postulate the creation of life spontaneously, by chance alone.

Evolutionary Theory of the Origin of Life

According to evolutionary theory, a few billion years ago the then-young earth had an atmosphere completely different from ours. It was an atmosphere without oxygen, containing methane, ammonia, hydrogen, and water vapor. By the action of ultraviolet rays, electrical discharges, and a continuous bombardment of highly charged particles, molecules were formed spontaneously and randomly. The molecules included sugars, amino acids, and pieces of DNA. More and more pieces clustered together and formed increasingly larger molecules and molecular chains. These giant molecules then combined until a primitive cell stage was reached, again, through a random process. Finally, those gelatinous clusters of proto-cells absorbed other molecules which, in combination with the gelatinous substances, at some point began to reproduce. Thus developed the first living cells. Those first living cells fed on the molecules still left in the "primeval soup."

Soon photosynthetic cells developed which produced and released into the atmosphere a necessary ingredient for virtually all life forms: oxygen. That oxygen, and the metabolism of those first living cells, destroyed the primitive molecules and changed the primeval atmosphere into the atmosphere as we know it. Once life had evolved, the earth's environment was so altered that life could no longer develop spontaneously on earth.

Christian writer Bernard Ramm summarizes this evolutionary model for the origin of life as follows:

"The origin of life on naturalistic premises is that life emerged through some fortunate situation in some primeval pool of water. It was not a sudden passage from the inorganic to the organic, but it was through a series of ever-increasing complex combinations, with many borderline combinations that would be half chemical and half living. Finally, true

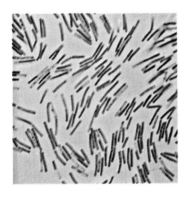

Right: In the late 1800s, Louis Pasteur proved that life cannot come from non-life.
Below: Even a "simple" bacterium contains a complicated amino acid structure. It is incredible that evolution postulates that all life, simple or complex, developed by chance.

protoplasm emerged, possessing the required properties to be defined as living. O. A. Oparin, *The Origin of Life* (1938), is one of the better attempts to explain the origin of life on a chemical basis. He surveys the condition of the earth from its proposed origin till the time when life could emerge. He tries to find the series of chemical bridges from the inorganic to life. It is refreshing that Oparin does not dogmatize, but labels his effort as speculatory, with many gaps in evidence. it is a treatise on how it might have occurred, not on how it actually did occur."[5]

What are the chances that life could have developed spontaneously in the hypothetical primeval soup by chance and over long periods of time? Take a simple bacterium. One single bacterium contains some 1,500 different enzymes, which in turn consist of several hundred amino acids. Those various amino acids must be arranged in precisely the right sequence. The chance that a given enzyme, consisting of two hundred amino acids (of which there are twenty different kinds) could develop by chance is one in 20^{200}. In other words, the chance is practically nil. And that is only one of the necessary 1,500 enzymes for *one* bacterium. The origin of a single living cell, then, would require billions of kilos of each of the many different enzymes and DNA molecules, combining and recombining randomly, until, against all probability, just the right random combination occurred.

The absurdity of believing such a scenario is described by scientist Henry M. Morris:

"The marvel of life can only be explained by creation. One of the strangest phenomena of our supposedly scientific age is the insistent faith held by many *scientists* (!) that somewhere, somehow life has arisen from non-life by naturalistic evolutionary processes. Science is supposed to be based on facts and knowledge, not speculation and wishful thinking. The law of biogenesis, based on all the *observed* data of biology and chemistry, states that life comes only from life. The doctrine of *abiogenesis*, on the other hand, teaches that certain unknown conditions in the primitive atmosphere and ocean acted upon certain mysterious chemicals existing at that time to synthesize still more complex chemicals which were able to reproduce themselves. These replicating chemicals, whatever they were, constituted the original living systems from which all living organisms later evolved.

"Thus, primeval *unknown* life forms which no longer exist were derived from *unknown* chemicals by *unknown* processes which no longer operate, in an atmosphere of exotic and *unknown* composition in contact with the primitive oceanic soup of *unknown* structure! This remarkable construct is today taught as sober *science* in our public schools, in spite of the fact that there is not one single scientific observation to demonstrate that such things ever happened or even could happen."[6]

Spontaneous Generation

A few centuries ago, people generally were convinced that life still developed spontaneously everywhere. This is known as the theory of spontaneous generation. It was believed, for example, that flies could develop from rotting meat. It took two centuries for the scientific opponents of this idea to convince everyone that life can come only from life. Numerous experiments showed that if the proper sanitary precautions were taken, such as preventing flies from laying eggs in the meat, no new life developed. Finally, Louis Pasteur took broth, thoroughly boiled it and then sealed it off to prevent contamination of new microbes. The broth stayed completely clear and sterile. There was no new life.

Proponents of spontaneous generation claimed that the proper nourishment from the air could not reach the broth, and that was why life did not develop in Pasteur's mixture. So Pasteur constructed a glass container that allowed air to circulate over the broth, but prevented microbes from reaching it. Again, the broth remained clear and sterile. The universally accepted scientific postulate became: Life cannot develop from nonliving matter.

What is truly curious is that the same scientists who so dogmatically support that postulate also believe that life did develop from nonlife several billions of years ago. Such scientists realize the inconsistency of assuming its past possibility while denying its present possibility. Their solution: conditions must have been radically different then from what they are now. It is important to note that there is no conclusive evidence that conditions then were radically different. Such a difference is merely a necessary presupposition, totally unverified by any evidence. And yet,

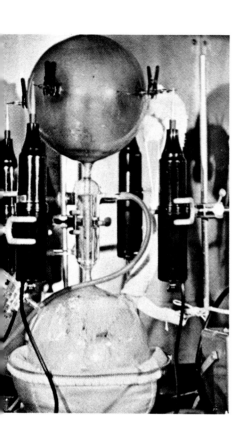

A portion of the laboratory apparatus used by Stanley L. Miller to create some of the basic building blocks of life.

60

most scientists and most introductory science texts present the existence of such a primeval soup and primeval atmosphere as fact.

What the scientists have done is illogical. They theorize that life came from nonlife. They backtrack from that and theorize that everything must have been very different when life came from nonlife. Then they say, "We have life today. That must prove that things were radically different and at that time life came from nonlife." The only fact the entire theory contains is that life exists today. They have done nothing unequivocally evidential to show either (1) that life came from nonlife or (2) that things were "radically different" enough for life to *have been able* to come from nonlife. Biologist L. Duane Thurman discusses the

The Viking landings on Mars discounted the possibility of life on that planet.

relationship of "spontaneous generation" to the origin of life in this way.

"Darwin spoke of life being breathed into one or more forms by the Creator. Most scientists today reject this and are attempting to synthesize life from inorganic chemicals in simulated prehistoric environments. Other scientists, however, claim this is not realistic since the Precambrian environment is not known and assumptions of its nature are often contradictory. In addition, the various compounds necessary for the synthesis require environments for their synthesis.

"The creation of living organisms from nonliving materials is spontaneous generation, an event which has been tried unsuccessfully for centuries. But, what if we do create life in a test tube? What will it tell us? For one thing, it will have been done by a designer, an intelligent being, and not by chance. And it will be an interesting, possible mechanism. But it will not tell us now life actually did originate. Such a simulated analysis would be only one explanation among several, including special creation.

"Why should scientists believe so firmly in spontaneous generation as the basic foundation for the whole theory, when it has not been demonstrated even once? Karl von Naegeli is probably closest to the truth when he says that 'to deny spontaneous generation is to proclaim a miracle.' This is one thing most scientists try to avoid. Emmel admits:

"Clearly, no biologist will ever know the complete story of the origin of life....A number of biologists feel that these hypotheses are compatible with a belief in a Supreme Deity; others hold to a purely mechanistic viewpoint. Neither point of view can be proved by physical evidence; thus research in this area is intellectually interesting and stimulating but without promise of a definitive answer."[7]

Life in a Test Tube?

During the 1950s, the work of scientist Stanley Miller attracted attention because he was attempting to create the simple building blocks of life, amino acids. To do that was a necessary preliminary to attempting to create life from nonlife in a laboratory setting. Miller duplicated the atmosphere that evolutionists had postulated as

The second law of thermodynamics mandates against the evolution of complex and living structures by random chance. On the contrary, we observe decay around us, not spontaneous creation.

providing the setting for the origin of life, and then he succeeded in producing certain molecules that are important building blocks of life. He accomplished that by subjecting the atmosphere of methane, ammonia, hydrogen, and water vapor to electrical charges. Then he immediately trapped the molecules that formed as a result of the reaction, since the electrical charges that cause the molecules to form would also disintegrate those molecules with their next charges. What most people failed to realize is that there was no such "trap" in the natural environment during the time of the origin of life, given the presupposition of random antisupernaturalism by macroevolutionists.

Miller's experiments not only produced molecules that are important building blocks for life, they also produced the biologically unusable "right-handed" molecules. Miller's experiments complicated rather than simplified matters for evolutionists. Did the primeval atmosphere also produce both kinds of molecules? If so, how did any life-building molecules dissociate themselves from the other molecules long enough to combine and produce the first living cell? And if the atmosphere was not the same as that in Miller's experiments, how do we know what it was and why it produced only life-building molecules? The problems with Miller's experiments proved greater than the solution he sought to provide for the origin of life.

We must also remember that Miller never produced one single living cell. He produced carefully guarded organic molecules, far removed from the complexity of a living cell.

Even if biochemists could succeed in producing something that resembles life or even is life, they still would not have proven that life originated spontaneously, as the result of random processes. Instead, they would have shown that life can be produced from matter and energy directed and controlled by intellectual effort and great technological skill. That is in accord with the biblical attribution of the creation of life to the greatest "scientist" of all—God. There has never been any other life, or materials like life, in any other part of the solar system that mankind has explored so far. Given the almost impossible

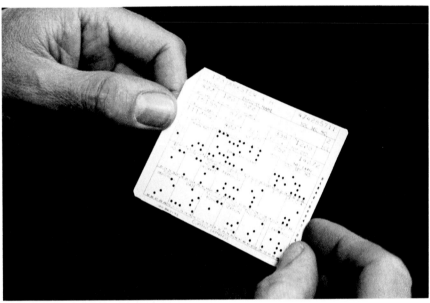

Right and below: Computer CPUs (Central Processing Units) can be compared to the complex data storage banks contained in the DNA of all living cells.

odds against life being produced spontaneously, and given that there is life here on earth, one's credibility is stretched to an extreme by evolutionists who would have us accept that there is life elsewhere in our universe. However, if life on this earth was the deliberate design and creation of God, then one easily can accept that God could have, just as easily, created life anywhere else in the universe he chose.

Bernard Ramm summarized the significance of Miller's experiments in this way:

"S. L. Miller, working under the direction of Harold Urey, performed an experiment in which he was able to synthesize amino acids with elements and conditions which supposedly represent the original conditions on the earth. In a closed system, water, methane, ammonia and hydrogen were heated so that they were vaporous and passed through a small electric corona discharge whose purpose was to simulate the radiation of the sun and the electrical phenomena of the primitive atmosphere. After a week the liquid was red and contained three types of amino acids which are the basic stuff of protein, and a number of unidentifiable, more complex compounds. Miller and Urey do not believe they have created life, but they feel they have made a significant start in the laboratory to unravel the problem of the origin of life.

"Harris has surveyed all the contemporary theories of the origin of life from non-living materials and finds them all defective. The six theories examined and rejected are that life originated by (i) spontaneous generation; (ii) from cosmic panspermia; (iii) from cell models; (iv) from colloids; (v) from enzymes; (vi) from viruses. Approaching the problem from a different perspective, Clark arrives at a similar negative judgment to Harris. He asserts that no definition of life or scientific explanation of its origin can stand up to criticism. The usual procedure is to explain one mystery by means of another. The fundamental criticism is that modern science works on the basis of a *scientific monism* by which he means that all there is is matter or substance or Nature. But, Clark continues, in that Nature operates on the grounds of *random activity* and the human intelligence on the principle of *organization and control*, we have a *final dualism*. A theistic explanation of the origin of life is the only possible explanation."[8]

Above: An artist's rendition of evolving life as it appeared during the Carboniferous period. Below: Britisher Thomas H. Huxley was a leading convert to and proponent of Darwin's theory of evolution.

How Does Entropy Relate to Evolution?

As we discussed before, one of the fundamental laws of the universe is that of *entropy*, or the second law of thermodynamics. Briefly stated, this means that in any general process, the amount of available or usable energy decreases or is less than what was available before the process. In cosmological terms this means that eventually the entire universe will cool, slow down, and be unable to use any more energy. Entropy means that random processes tend toward disorganization rather than organization, toward more randomness rather than more order. Bolton Davidheiser gives this as an illustration of entropy:

"When a spring-type clock is wound, energy is put into the spring as it is coiled tighter and tighter. As the spring uncoils, this energy operates the clock. But less energy is available for running the clock than was put into the spring during the winding because some of the energy dissipates as heat. In any operation, some energy is lost as heat or in some other way so that it is not useful to the process. Thus the total amount of useful energy becomes less. Scientists are certain that unless there is a creative force operating in the universe, a time will come when the sun and all the stars will burn out and the universe will have 'run down' completely.

"The 'running down' of the universe poses a real problem for the atheists, for how could it have gotten 'wound up' in the first place so that it can now be in the process of 'running down'? This is no problem at all for Christians, for the Bible says God created, and we are told that in the city of the New Jerusalem there will be no need for the sun or moon, for the glory of the Lord will light it. (See Revelation, chapter 21, especially verses 22 and 23.)"[9]

When we look at evolution, we see the problem evolutionists have with reconciling evolutionary theory with the law of entropy. The development of a living cell would require that nonliving matter spontaneously organize itself 'upward' to much higher degrees of order,

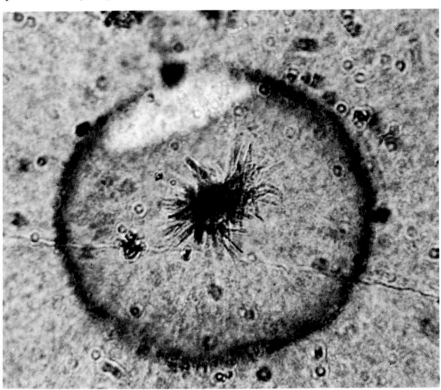

An egg, fertilized by a single sperm, contains all of the information necessary (in its DNA) to develop into an adult organism.

complexity, and purposefulness. But the second law of thermodynamics counters such a trend, evidencing instead that matter never increases in organization life.

Evolutionists, aware of the thermodynamic dichotomy, nonetheless believe in the spontaneous development of life. They attempt to reconcile the problem by objecting that the second law is applicable in a "closed system," i.e., a system that does not exchange or receive energy from outside itself. The earth, they maintain, is not a closed system. It is an open system which constantly receives abundant amounts of energy from the sun.

That, however, is a totally inadequate answer. Energy in and of itself contributes nothing to organization or design. Simply adding energy from the sun gives no developmental input to the random processes evolutionists describe for the origin of life. A pile of bricks and wood never would spontaneously develop into a building, no matter if the energy from the sun radiated on it for a trillion years. Matter and energy are insufficient causes of the complexity, design, and development we see around us.

Genesis 1:20-22 reads, "Then God said, 'Let the waters teem with swarms of living creatures, and let birds fly above the earth in the open expanse of the heavens.' And God created the great sea monsters, and every living creature that moves, with which the waters swarmed after their kind, and every winged bird after its kind; and God saw that it was good. And God blessed them, saying, 'Be fruitful and multiply, and fill the waters in the seas, and let birds multiply on the earth.'"

"Another way of looking at the second law of thermodynamics is that there is a trend toward randomness in the universe. That is, the trend is toward forming less complex distribution of matter and energy from more complex ones. A non-living structure left to itself tends to deteriorate and disintegrate. It falls apart and the pieces become scattered. A tornado can destroy a building, spreading its contents in a haphazard manner, but it will not assemble materials to form a building. The tendency toward randomness in nature is the opposite of evolution, for according to the theory of evolution, more complex forms have developed from less complex forms. Therefore it has been said that the theory of evolution is contrary to the second law of thermodynamics."[10]

What is lacking is a "program" to *organize* matter and energy into higher levels of order, complexity, and purposefulness. In order for a system to become more complex, it must have complexity added to it, not only energy. When Christians say that God is the Creator, they are asserting the Designer behind the design, the Intelligence behind the intelligence, the Purposer behind the purpose, and the Profundity behind the complexity of the universe. The heart of our argument, and the total defect in the evolutionary argument, is that Christians have an *adequate source* for the development and complexity in the universe, while evolutionists have *no adequate source* for the world they see around them.

"The second law of thermodynamics has not been discredited. The theory of evolution is very much in vogue today, and students and the general public are told over and over that its acceptance as a fact is practically unanimous among men of science. It follows from this that the evolutionists have been able to convince themselves that the theory of evolution is not contrary to this law. They do this by saying that there really is no contradiction because all the energy needed to bring about

Did man live when dinosaurs were alive? Perhaps so.
Above: A rock painting by the Fremont Indians of North America.
Right: A Mexican statue.
Below: Job's description of a strange animal (Job 40:15-24) is reminiscent of a Brontosaurus.

evolution has been supplied abundantly by an external source, namely the sun.

"A human being can overcome randomness and produce a more complex configuration by doing such things as taking pigments from various sources and arranging them to represent a landscape, or even by painting a sign saying, 'Keep off the grass.' To do these things requires intelligence, skill, and the expenditure of energy. It is evident that energy alone is not enough. A strong, young Eskimo given a pile of random letters might not be able to arrange any of them in such a way as to communicate a message.

"A bird can overcome randomness by collecting scattered materials and building a nest. This also requires an expenditure of energy, but energy alone is not enough. An ability which may be called an expression of instinct is also needed. As in the case of human beings, the energy comes from food, and it may be traced back to the sun as its origin."[11]

There once was a debate between evolutionist Thomas H. Huxley and Bishop Samuel Wilberforce. During the debate, Huxley took a pencil from his pocket and said, in essence, "I am convinced that, even as you were at one time as small as the point of this pencil and have developed into an adult, my remote ancestors were globs of slime the size of the point of this pencil and through the centuries developed into man." He meant that what happens on a small scale in the development of each human being can also happen on a large scale in evolution.

Huxley and evolutionary theory as a whole totally miss a vital element in the process of human development: No human egg cell will ever develop into anything, even a Huxley evolutionist, without a *program*, or design. In embryology that program is supplied by the genetic code. The components of a cell are totally disorganized and lacking any potential for development without the addition of a program. One cannot have development without a plan.

"An egg developing into an individual increases in complexity. This also requires an expenditure of energy, but again energy alone is not enough. An egg will not develop into a new individual unless it has a suitable genetic constitution to determine the pattern of the development.

"Thus more complex arrangements of matter can be produced from simpler or from random arrangements. In each of the examples given here, the energy required can be traced to an outside source, the sun. But in each case this energy was not enough. Such things as intelligence, skill, instinct, and genetic constitution were also required."[12]

The only reasonable conclusion to this section is that the presuppositions of macroevolutionary theory are contrary to the second law of thermodynamics. Evolutionists' attempts to reconcile the two, by factoring in energy from the sun, have failed. Energy is inadequate to account for the order, complexity, purpose, and design we see in the created world around us. On the other hand, to postulate a Designer, Orderer, and Purposer *outside* this system, God as the Creator, is both reasonable and consistent with the second law of thermodynamics.

The growth of giant trees like this contemporary Sequoia may have been common in the pre-flood, semi-tropical climate of the world.

Where Did Life Come From?

Our study in this chapter has made clear that life as we know it could not have evolved spontaneously or by chance, even given matter and energy. Evolution is incapable of accounting for the complexity and design everywhere evident in living organisms. Further, those evolutionists who take matter and energy, and to it add time, have still not answered the problem. Matter, energy, and time can accomplish no complexity on their own. What is needed is a designer or programmer. Christians know that Designer as the Lord God.

"At our present state of knowledge two things may be state. (i) Man has not produced life chemically. That he may produce protoplasmic specks [such as amino acids] is a possibility, but the production of even the smallest organism is as yet a long time away. In view of our inability to produce life with our vast chemical knowledge and our ability to reproduce almost any condition we wish of pressure, temperature or motion, we must still view a chance origin of life as a faith and not as a verified hypothesis. (ii) Unless a person is very anti-Christian it cannot be denied that the most satisfactory explanation to date is that life is the creation of the Living God. There is certainly nothing scientifically disrespectable in this connection, even though a person is not a believer. Those who do believe it, may do so without fear of contravening scientific fact and without prejudicing the character of their judgment.

"We conclude, then, that science is still unable to put forward any satisfactory explanation as to how life arose in the first place. We must either accept the Bible doctrine that God created life, or go on making improbable speculations."[13]

Following is a comparison of two common philosophical perspectives in interpreting the world and its origins.[14]

Nontheistic Evolutionist	Creationist
Naturalism	**Theism**
Nature is the sum total of reality. Knowledge of the world can be obtained entirely through the methods of science. There is no need to seek to explain the world in any other way.	Natural science is not sufficient by itself to provide answers to life's questions (1 Cor. 2:12-14). Part of reality can be explained only in spiritual terms (Jn. 4:24). A complete view of reality recognizes both the natural and supernatural aspects.
Uniformity	**Sovereignty**
The Uniform Process Theory states that knowledge of the present is sufficient to explain the past and to predict the future. This is done on the basis of certain natural laws which are said to be changeless. There is no divine intervention in history.	The world was created by God (Heb. 11:3; Gen. 1:1; 2 Pet. 3:5-6). God does not change and has created a world which obeys certain uniform natural laws (Heb. 13:8; Prov. 3:19-20). But the history of the universe is not explicable in terms of natural laws alone because God is not bound by those laws (Mt. 19:26).
Chance (Causalism)	**Purpose (Teleology)**
Life began as the result of chance events. The end result of a chance event is a consequence rather than the achievement of a purpose. Because the present forms of life originated by chance, they could easily have arisen in some other form or not at all.	The world was created by God for His purpose. All history is a working out of God's plan (Col. 1:16-17; Eph. 1:9-12). Mankind was made in the image of God's own divine personality (Gen. 1:26; Rom. 8:28-29).

CHAPTER FIVE

Evolution or Creation

Charles Darwin, the "father" of modern evolutionary theory, was born on February 12, 1809, at Shrewsbury (country of Shropshire, England). Although modern evolutionary theory is much more sophisticated than what Darwin devised, his name is still the one that for most people evokes immediate ideas of the "ape-to-man" theory. In this chapter we will discuss what evolution is, how the theory was developed, and how it contrasts with *biblical creationism*.

Some readers may be surprised to learn that not everything labeled with the title "evolution" is necessarily opposed to Christianity. For example, some Christians in science regard themselves as "theistic evolutionists"—although the present author does not regard "theistic evolution" as a biblically tenable position. In contrast, other well-qualified, intelligent scientists reject macroevolution in favor of the biblical creation account. Although we will not exhaust the study of the evolution/creation controversy in these few pages, we will try to provide a general background to the subject, along with some useful ways of looking at the controversy, from angles both scientific and biblical.

Left: Charles Darwin: the founder of the modern evolutionary theory. This painting was done by John Collier in 1883 (after Darwin's death).
Right: A model of the Beagle, the ship on which Darwin sailed during the five years of research which resulted in his general theory of evolution.

Life of Charles Darwin

Charles Darwin's grandfather, Erasmus Darwin, postulated a primitive theory of evolution before Charles was born; these theories (largely

71

rejected at the time) were even then called "Darwinism." Now that term refers to the grandson's more sophisticated system, which he began to develop on his five-year voyage on the *Beagle* as the staff naturalist. Charles began his university studies in medicine, following in his physician father's footsteps. Then he changed his major to theology, looking forward to enjoying life as a quiet country clergyman in the Anglican Church. At Cambridge Darwin studied geology with Professor Adam Sedgwick and botany with Professor John Stevens Henslow. When his theological studies did not inspire him sufficiently to seek a pastorate after graduation, he returned to his father's house with few concrete plans for the future. On Henslow's recommendation, young Darwin

Right: Monk Gregor Mendel (1822-1884), whose studies of plant reproduction and genetics became important to evolutionary theory. Below: A microscope used by Mendel.

was offered a post as botanist on the sailing vessel *Beagle*, which was embarking on a five-year voyage to prepare more accurate navigational charts. During that voyage, which began in 1831, Darwin's religious beliefs were replaced by a general materialism, which undoubtedly influenced his developing thesis of nontheistic evolution. Bolton David-heiser quotes Darwin's description of his loss of religious belief:

"I had gradually come by this time to see that the Old Testament from its manifestly false history of the world...was no more to be trusted than the sacred books of the Hindus, or the beliefs of the barbarian.... I gradually came to disbelieve in Christianity as a divine revelation."[1]

As preparation for his duties aboard the *Beagle*, Darwin studied the newly published first volume of Lyell's *Principles of Geology*, which popularized what is called the uniformitarian view. The uniformitarian view postulated that the natural agencies for geological change which we observe around us today are the same types and intensities of agencies that have worked for geological change throughout the history of the earth. Local floods, earthquakes, landslides, etc., all occurred throughout the history of the earth and accounted for the variety of geological evidence we see today.[2]

The part of his journey that had the most impact on Darwin's budding

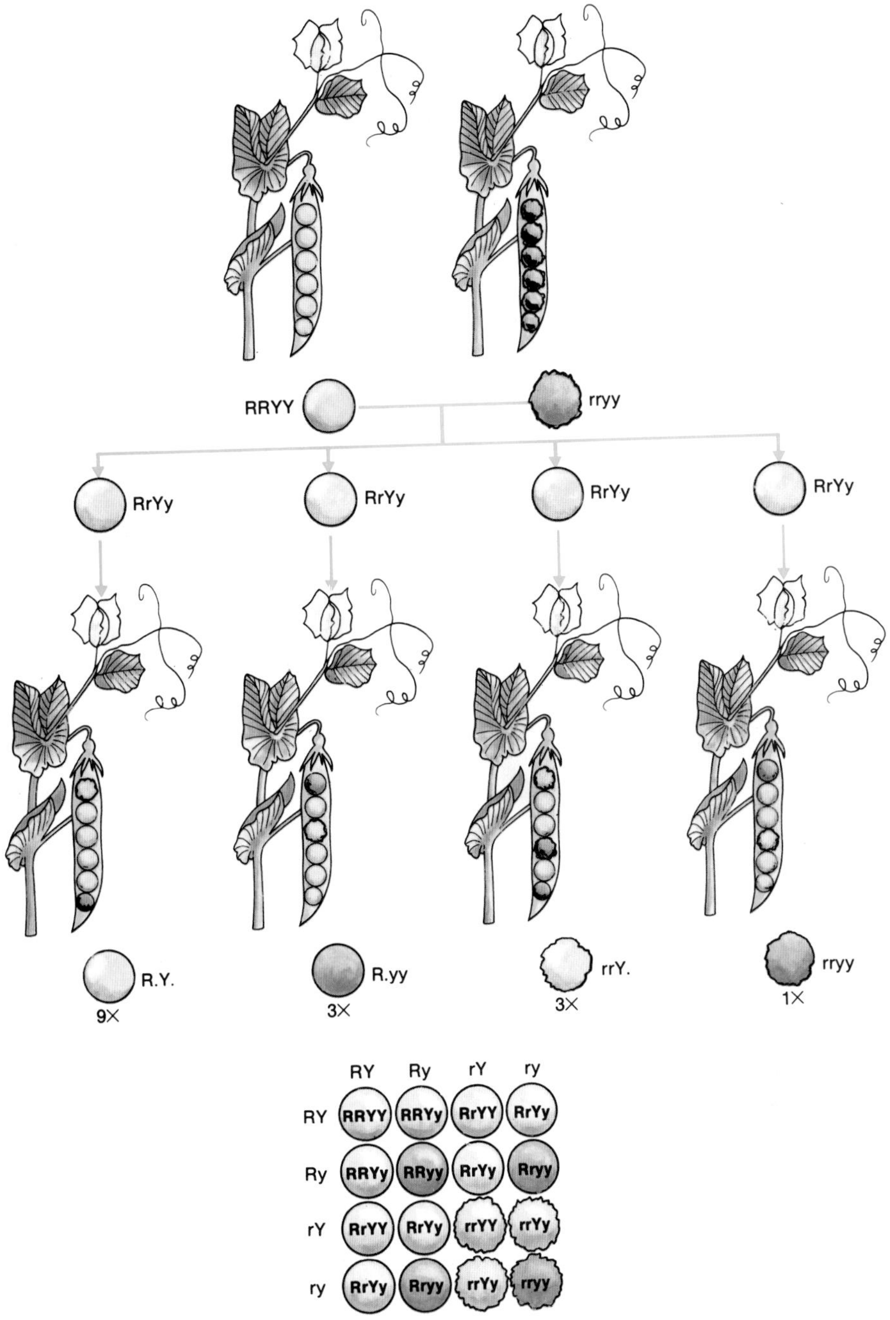

This chart illustrates the hereditary characteristics of the peas (R, round; and Y, yellow) with which Mendel experimented.

RRYY | rryy

RrYy | RrYy | RrYy | RrYy

R.Y. 9× | R.yy 3× | rrY. 3× | rryy 1×

	RY	Ry	rY	ry
RY	RRYY	RRYy	RrYY	RrYy
Ry	RRYy	RRyy	RrYy	Rryy
rY	RrYY	RrYy	rrYY	rrYy
ry	RrYy	Rryy	rrYy	rryy

evolutionary scheme was the time the ship spent in the region of the Galapagos Islands, off the west coast of South America. There Darwin observed finches that were similar to mainland finches, but enough different that they were unable to interbreed with mainland birds or even with birds on neighboring islands. Later Darwin used these finches as examples of adaptive evolution, a microcosm of the grand evolutionary design by which he believed all life had developed to its current complexity.

Darwin believed that the finches had been blown by storm winds from the mainland to the islands and there developed significant differences through isolation and interbreeding.

"The idea is that the birds got to the islands accidentally from the mainland, by the action of a storm or some freak of nature, and developed differently because they were isolated on separate islands. It

An example of the large evening primrose (Oenothera erythrosepala). Hugo de Vries (below) discovered different characteristics among different varieties of primroses, which appeared to him to support the evolutionary theory.

is strange indeed, though apparently overlooked for convenience, that they would accidentally cross hundreds of miles of ocean and then remain isolated on small islands within sight of each other. If a storm carried them so far to sea, it is to be expected that sooner or later other storms would mix them up on the islands. William Beebe, the noted naturalist, did not believe the birds came to the islands by accident from South America, but that they came by way of a former land bridge from Central America."[3]

Darwin did not publish his complete theory of evolution until he was fifty years old. The theory was described in *The Origin of Species by Means of Natural Selection or the Preservation of Favored Races in the Struggle for Life* (1859). It is interesting to note that another Englishman, Alfred Russel Wallace (1823-1913) promoted the same type of theory at the same time Darwin was promoting his. The two, Wallace and Darwin, even published joint papers in an 1858 journal. That Darwin's work became famous and shaped evolutionary thought over a century after its first publication is testimony to his greater persuasive ability and his more thorough and carefully thought-out work. Darwin also provided much more extensive data from field observations than did Wallace.

Darwin died in 1882, years after the first furor over his revolutionary new scientific postulates had died down. He spent the last third of his

life refining, defending, and promoting his general theory of evolution. We will survey his theory below.

Darwin's Evolutionary Theory

Darwin's general theory of evolution, as first described in his *Origin of Species*, can be summarized in six points (here somewhat simplified).

First, Darwin recognized, as all observant people and scientists would, that species differ. Second, Darwin observed that the mortality rate among the infants of species was extremely high, and appeared to be compensated for by large numbers of births. Third, Darwin proposed his now-famous "struggle for existence" theory: that offspring struggle

Above and right: The great variety of plant life found throughout the world, under diverse and often harsh climatic conditions, is testimony to the intricate creative design of God.

to be of the survivor class instead of dying. Fourth, given that this struggle exists, it stands to reason that those individuals who survive must be more fit than those who die. This Darwinian concept is usually referred to as "survival of the fittest." Fifth, Darwin assumed that fit individuals who also reproduced passed on the genetic characteristics that had made them better able to survive to their offspring. Sixth, Darwin concluded by describing his basic evolutionary theory: New species arise by the continued survival and reproduction of the individuals best fitted or adapted to their own particular environment.[4]

Most reasonable people would not disagree with all of Darwin's points; one cannot really argue with the first two. There are many species, and most populations produce more offspring than actually survive to maturity. There is strong disagreement, however, even among non-Christian scientists, as to whether there is a true "struggle" for existence of the sort Darwin deemed vital to his basic conclusions. It is also generally not true that only the fittest survive. John W. Klotz refers to this early and persistent criticism of Darwin's theory:

"There are also many instances in which the fittest individual does not survive. Often the survival of one individual and the death of another is a matter of chance. This criticism of Darwin's theory was pointed out very early. It may be that one individual is not exposed to the same environmental stresses as another member of the same species. In this way he may survive, even though he may not be as fit as his less fortunate neighbor. This is especially true where animals are the victims of predators. Here it is often a matter of chance which individual supplies the predator with his dinner. Defenders of Darwin have pointed out that not all deaths are due to elimination by chance, and they base their theory on that portion of the cases in which natural selection rather than chance is the factor involved. It should, however, be pointed out that this does reduce the number of cases to which natural selection applies and that it increases the chance of the elimination of the fit individual."[5]

Right: An illustration of the postulated Jurassic Sea, in which are seen a number of dinosaur types.
Below: All species of dog, including this beagle, are variations from the original dogs created by God.

Finally (and because of space limitations our comments again are circumscribed), the most significant problem with Darwin's theory is his assumption or conclusion that fitness characteristics are passed on to an individual's descendants. Many different characteristics might make an individual more fit than another of the same species group. However, some of those characteristics usually do *not* represent *genetic*, or inheritable, characteristics. As a simple example, we could think of an Olympic runner. While some portion of his fitness for running could be genetic and therefore inheritable (being born with large lung capacity, etc.), the most significant factor in his achieving Olympic status is what he *does* with his "raw materials." Large lung capacity is totally irrelevant if he never uses it, but instead whiles away his time lying on the couch watching television. Many of his runner's advantages arise from training, self-discipline, and hard work. Such factors are not genetic and are not inheritable. Although he may produce a child who also is a great runner, just as possibly he may not.

We conclude our section on Darwin by remarking that, although he produced a comparatively well-researched and well-thought-out proposal, it is reasonable to take issue with some of his most important propositions and conclusions. His theory has consequently undergone many modifications.

Gregor Mendel, the Father of Genetics

A contemporary of Darwin was an Augustinian monk, Gregor Mendel. His experiments on inheritance (conducted at his monastery in what is now Brno, Czechoslovakia) began with the crossbreeding of numerous varieties of garden peas.

In 1856 Mendel began making careful observations of peas he raised on a small plot in the monastery garden. Nine years later, in 1865, Mendel reported his findings to the local scientific society. He reported that when different varieties of peas are crossed, the hereditary characteristics of each variety are not lost in the hybrid, but will reappear in

Right: A fox.
Below: A wolf.
The Bible does not provide enough information for us to know whether all dog types, including the fox and the wolf, developed from an original dog type or were created separately by God.

subsequent generations of the hybrid. That reappearance will occur in a mathematically predictable manner. Regrettably, the local society failed to see the potential significance of Mendel's work. Then, Mendel himself was forced to abandon his experiments because of other responsibilities, and he died in 1884, little recognized for what later became known as *Mendel's laws.*

Even though Mendel's work was unappreciated during his lifetime, three scientists, de Vries (Holland), Correns (Germany), and von Tschermak (Austria) independently worked with Mendel's conclusions in 1900 and brought Mendel's name and work to worldwide attention and recognition.

Hugo de Vries — the Mutation Theory

The best known of the three re-workers of Mendel's theories was a Dutch scientist, Hugo de Vries. His work concerning mutations is still used by many evolutionists today. In 1905 de Vries published his now well-known *Species and Varieties, Their Origin by Mutation.* This book described his work with a species of evening primrose, *Oenothera lamarckiana.* He cultivated several previously wild varieties and produced what he called a completely new species. His work and popularization of Mendel's studies awakened great scientific interest in the study of genetics.

De Vries was convinced by his work that new species arise by beneficial mutations which are then passed down through successive generations. However, many scientists today agree that the different kinds of plants produced in de Vries's experiments were not representative of actual new species but were just varieties of the same species. In addition, his theory was open to even more severe criticism, as Klotz notes:

"However, the new 'species' of de Vries were not species, but rather varieties — varieties, to be sure, which were quite different, but nevertheless only varieties. Moreover, most, if not all, of de Vries' 'mutations' were not mutations as we know them today, but were due to the breeding out of recessive characters present in the stock but not showing themselves (similar to the birth of an albino child to two normal parents both of whom are 'carriers' of the trait) and to

Right: The ox, the sheep, the goat, gazelle all belong to the one family, Bovidae.
Below: Some "Genesis kinds" can interbreed, such as the rat and the mouse.

chromosomal rearrangements within the cells....

"Today we do see mutations in various plants and animals. These are sudden, abrupt changes in the organism which are due to changes in the genes. They are inherited, and hence are passed down from generation to generation. For instance, in the latter part of the eighteenth century there appeared in a purebred New England flock of sheep a lamb with very short, bowed legs. This lamb was bred and gave rise to the Ancon breed of sheep. It is obvious that this character would be one desirable to the breeder. Such an animal cannot jump fences and cannot run fast and thus lose weight. Incidentally, it is also obvious that such a character is unfavorable to the sheep. Such a sudden inheritable variation is known as a mutation.

"There have been literally thousands of such mutations, some striking and signicant, and others insignificant. Like the Ancon mutation in the sheep, however, most of these mutations have proved to be harmful to the organism."[6]

In concluding our section on Darwin, Mendel, and de Vries, it is important to note that the modern general theory of evolution is that natural selection and genetic manipulation (through breeding and/or mutations) are the basic mechanisms by which change and development are accomplished. Evolution, in that view, is the general cause of

Right: A cross between a zebra and a horse. Such mating is possible, but the offspring is sterile.
Below: A breeding colony of pelican-like birds.

all development and differentiation among plant and animal life throughout the history of life on earth.

Terminology

Before we give the contrasting views of evolution and creation, we should define some of the terms we are using. Much of the conflict between the evolution and creation views arises because both evolutionists and creationists tend to misunderstand what the other is saying.

Evolution generally means a process of change in a certain direction. When we refer to evolution in the history of earthly life, we mean that life as we know it today has come through a process (and is still in that process) of development from simple to more complex, single to multiple, "lower" to "higher" forms of life. It is important to remember that competent scientists use the term *evolution* also to describe a variety of lesser degrees of change. Some scientists use evolution to refer to what most people think of as individual variations within a "family" grouping of a particular species. Scientists also use evolution as descriptive of small change among different families, or populations, within a species (things like different populations with different dominant colorings, etc.). Those smaller changes are often referred to as *microevolution*. Finally, evolution can refer to our initial definition above, where there is change from one species to another, or changes in other major categories of organisms. Such major change is often referred to as *macroevolution*. It is also important to understand the terms *species* and *mutation*. In further discussion, in fact, we will find that some evolutionary arguments fall because of a faulty understanding of what a species is or what a mutation is. Duane Thurman has a good, concise definition of "species" which takes into account several variations on one definition:

"A species is a basic unit of classification which can be recognized and placed in a classification system without even considering evolution. The concept originated independent of evolutionary theory. It is defined in several different ways, depending upon the backgrounds and purposes of the investigators. Some, such as Linnaeus, defined a species

Genetic manipulation of African violets produces interesting hereditary results. Radiation exposure is especially effective in such manipulation and may be a clue to radiation exposure at times in earth's history.

as a group of individuals which looked alike. He said that there was an unbridged gap (that is, a lack of common characteristics) between species. Mayr defines it genetically as 'groups of interbreeding populations that are reproductively isolated from other such groups.'

"Some say that a species is just a concept, the product of each scientist's judgment, while others say a species is a reality of nature. This wide range of opinion on definitions might be summarized by saying that 'it is increasingly clear that no single definition of species can be devised to express all the actual meanings of the word.' A species may be characterized in several different ways, but most definitions agree on the following: a species has certain designated characteristics in common; it usually does not interbreed with other species in nature; and if members of one species do breed with members of another, they usually will not produce fertile offspring.

"Some situations in nature are so complex that it is largely a matter of personal judgment whether to consider the populations as one species with several varieties or as one genus with several species. In any case, it is important to determine what any author's definition of species is, especially when he or she is writing about the formation of new species."[7]

Most scientists agree on the basic definition of a *mutation:* an abrupt change in the genetic code of an individual which can then be passed on to successive generations (as either a dominant or recessive trait). Disagreement occurs, however, when one discusses the significance of mutations in (1) the development of new varieties and/or species and in (2) whether a particular "new" characteristic is the result of a true mutation. It is not an unobserved normal genetic trait, or even an acquired characteristic.

Mutations are important to evolutionists because the presence of mutations often is used to account for a small divergent group within a species being able to survive and adapt to a hostile change in the host environment. We must remember, however, that the vast majority of

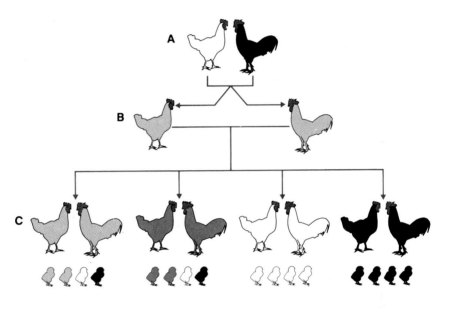

While Mendel's experiments revealed hereditary patterns, there is no strict demarcation between dominant and recessive characteristics, as illustrated by this diagram of chicken breeding.

mutations observed in the laboratory and field are harmful mutations. Far from promoting survival, they most often ensure the demise of the affected individuals. Thurman concludes:

"Mutations produce widely varying kinds and amounts of change. Some changes are so drastic that the organism dies during the early stages of development. Others will survive but die early because of severe deformity or malfunction. Consequently, most mutations available for study consist of small effects (micromutations) which are not serious handicaps to the development and survival of the individual. This is the commonest type of mutation referred to by both evolutionists and creationists."[8]

We would add that such minute mutations seem completely inadequate to account for macroevolution because they produce only increasing variety but not increasing complexity.

The Evolutionary Picture

By *macroevolution* is meant the process by which simple organisms developed into complex organisms over a long period of time, transforming primitive life forms into the complex and varied life forms in our world today. If we were to draw a word picture of macroevolution, it would be described something like this.

We start with the primitive, nonliving early earth environment. Macro-evolutionists assume that nonliving things developed into living things —even though spontaneous generation violates "natural law." (See chapter four for further information on the origin of life.) Since they believe that all living forms in evidence today developed from common original ancestors, macroevolutionists must assume that all plants and animals (and viruses and bacteria) are somehow germinally related. Macroevolutionists see the progress of evolution as a sort of tree or family lineage, with just a few main branches. For example, all of the invertebrates are related; they represent an ancient part of the tree of

Above and below: The British moth (Biston bistularia) *adapted to its changing environment by the greater survival rate of those offspring whose color successfully hid them. This adaptation, or variation within a species, is not evidence for general evolution.*

life. From the invertebrates developed the vertebrates, all of whom are closely interrelated (and related by ancestry to the invertebrates). Finally, macroevolutionists divide the vertebrates into their own chronologically occurring "families" of amphibians, reptiles, birds, and mammals. This is what is often referred to as the "General Theory of Evolution."

What is truly fascinating about macroevolutionists is that they describe this tree in detail and yet have no hard evidence of its actual development. Almost all aspects of the general theory are supported only by inference or by interpreting the data with the presupposition that evolution is already an established fact. Thurman points out this inconsistency in the scientific method of evolutionists:

... "They assume that a certain series of events has occurred in the past. Thus though it may be possible to mimic some of these events under present-day conditions, this does not mean that these events must therefore have taken place in the past. All that it shows is that it is *possible* for such a change to take place. Thus to change a present-day reptile into a mammal, though of great interest, would not show the way in which the mammals did arise. Unfortunately, we cannot bring about even this change; instead we have to depend upon limited circumstantial evidence for our assumptions...."[9]

Left and above: While mutations are heralded often as fortuitous tools of evolutionary change, almost all of them are harmful or useless mutations. Mutations cannot account for evolution.

To summarize the most important features of and the contrasts between the evolutionary model and the creation model, we reproduce below a concise chart.[10]

CREATION MODEL	EVOLUTION MODEL
By acts of a Creator.	By naturalistic mechanistic processes due to properties inherent in inanimate matter.
Creation of basic plant and animal kinds with ordinal characteristics complete in first representatives.	Origin of all living things from a single living source which itself arose from inanimate matter. Origin of each kind from an ancestral form by slow gradual change.
Variation and speciation limited within each kind.	Unlimited variation. All forms genetically related.

Using our definitions, models, and survey of evolutionary thought, we will turn now to a discussion of the testimony of genetics concerning evolution and creation.

Does genetic evidence support the idea that hybrids are possible within

Mangroves growing on lava rocks in the Galapagos Islands, where Darwin made the most important observations which led him to postulate the general theory of evolution.

certain groups of plants and animals; can new species develop, which are clearly defined and separated from other similar groups? That would be consistent with creation. Or, does genetic evidence support the possibility of the formation of new species *ad infinitum*, and across the boundaries of existing groups? That would be consistent with evolution.

The findings of genetics do not point in the direction of evolution, but rather that the families must have come into being independently of each other. Molecular genetics especially has provided strong support for this conclusion. Molecular research has brought to light certain kinds of "shifts" in the relationship of genetic factors. Such shifts can form the basis of the development of new species (i.e., within a family — which is consistent with the biblical account). Nowhere, however, have scientists been able to observe consistent and major sequences of genetic changes that would mirror macroevolutional development in the past. In fact, the most significant and species-changing genetic trends are usually produced artificially by the direct intervention of humans who interbreed and hybridize plants and other organisms for various purposes. The deliberate manipulation of genetic material for a designed end does not reflect blind chance and random development. On the contrary, if anything, it reflects the direction and design of a Creator. Gish summarizes this point:

"It must be strongly emphasized, also, that in all cases these specialized breeds possess reduced viability; that is, their basic ability to survive has been weakened. Domesticated plants and animals do not compete well with the original, or wild type. Thus, Falconer has stated:

Our domesticated animals and plants are perhaps the best demonstration of the effects of this principle. The improvements that have been made by selection in these have clearly been accompanied by a reduction of fitness for life under natural conditions, and only the fact that domesticated animals and plants do not live under natural conditions has allowed these improvements to be made.

Right: One of the many varieties of finches. Observation of Galapagos finch varieties contributed to Darwin's theories. Below: Darwin as a young man.

"These experiments thus demonstrate that even with the aid of man's inventive genius, which permits the maximum variation in the shortest possible time, the variation achieved is extremely limited and actually results in plants and animals with reduced viability. They survive only because they are maintained in an environment which is free from their natural enemies, food supplies are abundant, and other conditions are carefully regulated."[11]

Species Development and the Genesis Account of Creation

We do not believe that the biblical account of creation denies any change in species as the result of human intervention or selective adaptation or crossbreeding. That is neither the intent nor the vocabulary of Genesis. When Genesis 1 states that God created the plants and animals to reproduce "after their own *kind*," it does not mean that the species types and limits are always inviolate. The Genesis word *kind* is a general term, having application in different contexts to species, families, orders, classes, or phyla. Klotz discusses the Hebrew term in Genesis and its relationship to the scientific term species:

"We shall have to agree that the Bible does not use the term 'species.' The Hebrew word used is *min*, which is probably best translated 'kind.' The word does not mean species in the same sense that we use the term today....

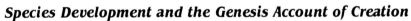

"Accepting the definition of species given [previously], we shall certainly have to admit that there have been new species. We cannot go along with Linnaeus who said: '*Species tot sunt, quot formae ab initio creatae sunt*' (there are as many species as there are forms created in the beginning). True, most of the demonstrable instances have arisen in very artificial situations and under laboratory conditions, so that it is unlikely that they could have arisen in that way out in nature. Nevertheless they are new species in the generally accepted sense of the term. And it is not correct to say that no new species have arisen since Creation."[12]

Understanding the linguistic parameters of the Genesis *kind* and the ambiguity in scientific classification systems removes the artificial dichotomy between *limited speciation* and *special creation*. Thurmond comments:

"Some creationists consider the famous fossil horse series as evidence for microevolution, not macroevolution. The changes are all within the horse 'kind' and are similar to those found today in living horses. Admitting that this amount of change occurs within a kind does not require accepting the entire theory of macroevolution."[13]

Conclusion

We will conclude our survey of evolution and creation by stating that there is no direct evidence of the macroevolution proposed by scientists who presuppose a naturalistic and mechanistic world. On the contrary, many pieces of evidence pointed to by evolutionists often can be used by creationists to support the creation model. Lack of space precludes our discussing in depth the vast controversy between evolution and creation. We refer the reader to the recommended reading for further information. Thurman provides a cogent summary for our present discussion:

"Recent research still has not produced the evidence called for...The evolutionist crosses these gaps by faith in evolution in the same way that a creationist crosses the gaps by faith in God. It is not a matter of whether or not one has faith, because either choice requires it. It should be understood that the object of faith is one of the biggest differences between evolutionists and creationists."[14]

CHAPTER SIX

The Testimony of the Fossils

An artist's concept of plant and dinosaur life during the Cretaceous period.

Over the last 150 years, scientists have found and catalogued millions of fossils (remains of plants and animals). Many fossils are records of plants and animals that are now extinct. Many others are identical to plants and animals alive today. Fossils are scattered through many different rock formations, sometimes in small concentrations, sometimes packed densely on one another. Klotz gives a good description of fossils:

"Let us look first at the fossils. These are the hard parts of plants and animals which have been preserved by petrification. Sometimes bones and teeth are preserved by having their pores filled with mineral matter, and in this case the hard material of the bone or tooth remains intact and unaltered. In other cases the original substance of the hard part is dissolved away and replaced, often particle by particle, by mineral matter, such as silica or carbonate of lime. Wood is commonly preserved in this way, and the process may be so delicate that the cells and other microscopic structures of the wood are preserved even after all the organic matter has disappeared."[1]

Evolutionists assume that the rock strata (layers) containing these fossils developed very gradually over a period of millions of years. For a fossil to form from a dead organism, that organism must be preserved from corruption by forces of decay that would otherwise disintegrate it

87

long before its physical components could be replaced, almost molecule by molecule, by mineral (rock) deposits. That so many millions of plants and animals were preserved this way is truly remarkable. Some fossils represent the entire organism, even its soft parts, which would typically decay long before calcification could take place. How did that remarkable preservation take place? And how do we account for the huge deposits of fossils which seem almost like mass graves because of the abundance of fossils?

Millions of years of evolution seem unable to account for them, but cataclysmic forces (including local isolated catastrophes as well as the cataclysmic flood), wiping out whole populations at one time, would be consistent with the fossil records we find. Henry Morris comments:

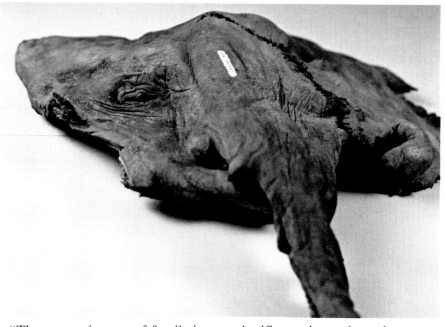

Right: A young mammoth, frozen so quickly that even his soft flesh has been preserved.
Below: Strict uniformitarianism must explain the mass fossil beds scattered around the world, reminiscent of mass graves.

"The very existence of fossils in any significant size and number seems to require rapid processes of sedimentary deposition, burial, compaction, and lithification. Otherwise, normal decay processes would soon destroy and dissipate such organic remains.

"Furthermore, the fossil record does not show a continuous evolutionary progression at all, as the theory requires. The same great gaps between the major kinds of plants and animals that exist in the present world are also found in the fossil world. Of course many animals that once lived have become extinct (such as the dinosaurs); but extinction is not evolution!"[2]

Klotz confirms Morris's assessment of the fossil enigma. He offers a theory of fossilization consistent with the creation model:

"For one thing, immediate burial is a first prerequisite for fossilization, and it should be such as to exclude the air so as to prevent oxidation of the organism. Usually this burial is effected by water-borne sediment, so that fossil remains of creatures making their homes in the shallower regions of the seas, rivers, and lakes are the most common. Thus the record is not truly representative of all habitats. Deep sea organisms are comparatively unknown, because so little of these deposits have been elevated onto land. Deposits formed near the mouths of rivers sometimes contain the remains of land animals, but these inclusions are

purely accidental and, like the fossils of deep sea organisms, not too common. Wind-borne materials, such as loess or volcanic ash, sometimes yield fossils of land-living animals, and miring in bogs and quicksands has also provided fossils of land animals. Yet they are still relatively uncommon."[3]

Many fossil beds could have been formed through catastrophic means rather than by the "thousands of years in the making" evolutionary explanation. In a cave in Maryland, fossil remains of dozens of different mammals were found, together with those of many reptiles and birds. These fossils represent animals from tropical, moderate, and polar regions together in one "grave." In Germany there are lignite beds (a

Right: This fossilized young stegosaurus skeleton is part of the mass dinosaur fossil deposit at Utah's Dinosaur National Monument.
Below: Fish fossils are numerous in most parts of the earth. Sometimes the preservation is remarkable, the fossil showing no sign that the body had begun decomposing.

form of brown coal) containing large numbers of fossil plants, animals, and insects from various regions and climates of the world. The remarkable preservation of the detailed structures and even the chemical contents of these animals is striking proof of sudden burial.

The Baltic amber deposits contain fossilized insects and plants from a wide variety of climates. The gathering of such a variety is consistent with the idea of a large and sudden catastrophe. Near Lompoc, California, enormous diatomite deposits were found containing millions of beautifully preserved fossil fish, usually in a position indicating sudden death. Masses of fossilized fish have also been found in Scotland. Seventy tons of dinosaur fossils were found in China at an altitude of 4,000 meters. How did they get that high?

The fossilization of such large organisms as dinosaurs and whole trees presents another problem to the traditional evolutionary approach to fossilization. These gigantic fossils frequently have been found complete and intact. Yet organisms of that size could never have been fossilized if they had been covered slowly. They would have decayed first. We must conclude that they were covered almost immediately, as with sand and water. For example, there is a fossilized tree trunk eighteen meters long with a diameter of almost two meters at its base, found at an angle of forty degrees in a coal mine in Newcastle, England. The trunk rises through ten separate layers of coal. It is difficult to imagine the porportions of a cataclysm that could account for such an anomaly. Although local traps such as California's La Brea Tar Pits can account for some of these giant fossils, their abundance precludes such a simplistic explanation for all of them.

"Perhaps the most remarkable instance of organisms mired in bogs and quicksands is the death trap found in the Rancho La Brea on the western border of Los Angeles. Here oils have distilled under the influence of sun and wind to form a viscous asphalt in which even large mammals, such as mastodons and saber-toothed cats have been trapped. It appears that the trapping of one mammal acted as a bait to attract various carnivores, which have themselves been trapped."[4]

Coal and the Evolutionary Time Scale

Coal is a mineral resulting from decomposed vegetation that has been subjected to great heat and pressure. Typically, evolutionists ascribe coal layers to successive deposits. Each layer of coal represents a period during which the land sank, so that marshes and peat bogs were formed. Later, the plant mass was covered by sediment and the land rose again, after which the process repeated itself. Thousands of years are needed to account for the enormous coal beds scattered around the world.

There are many peat bogs today, but as far as can be observed, none is the top of an uninterrupted series of coal beds. The peat bog theory is not confirmed by what is observable today. Henry Morris summarizes the creation model explanation of coal beds:

"The great coal beds of the world are recognized not as the accumulations of age after age of peat-bog growth, but rather as the transported and metamorphosed remains of the extensive and luxuriant vegetation of the antediluvian world. The oil reservoirs are the traps into which the compressed and converted remains of millions of buried marine animals have migrated after burial in the subterranean upheavals of the 'fountains of the great deep.'"[5]

Coal layers occasionally split into two layers, separated by water-deposited sediments. Marine fossils (worms, corals, mollusks, etc.) are frequently found in the midst of coal beds. In an evolutionary scheme such finds are anomalous, but in a catastrophic (flood) scheme they are consistent. The most curious aspect of coal beds is their great number. In India, for example, fifty to sixty layers of coal are stacked, one on top of another, some as thick as thirty meters, in a repeated cycle of coal, sandstone, and shale (former clay). As many as seventy-six layers have been found in Nova Scotia, eighty in England, and up to one hundred layers at an enormous bed in Germany. It stretches one's credibility to postulate that the same land mass rose and fell eighty to one hundred times in a given area, and that each time new peat bogs were formed.

It is much more consistent to interpret the data according to a catastrophic model—that is, as layers of vegetation killed and destroyed by flooding, covered with sand and then clay, and then receiving subsequent inundations. Such a pattern would be consistent with the Genesis flood in Noah's time. It is also consistent with the enormous pressure and heat necessary to form coal. Laboratory research has shown that wood can be transformed into coal in less than one hour when high pressure and temperature are applied.

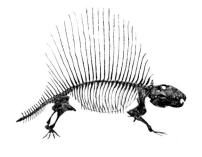

An Edaphosaurus, *whose long vertebrae extensions may have allowed for efficient skin cooling.*

Above: A fossilized tree trunk (dendrolite), often found in coal beds.
Right: The fossil-bearing strata which are considered to be the oldest contain remains of marine life, such as these marine animals called sea lillies.
Below: Coal beds are actually vast plant deposits.

Fossils "According to Their Kinds"

According to the theory of evolution, all life forms have developed gradually and progressively, one from another. The fossil record does not support that. In nature there are a number of well-defined main groups of plants and animals without intermediate forms clearly linking them. The fossil record shows the same gaps, in spite of the fact that, according to evolution, all organisms, living or dead (fossilized), represent a continuous "tree" development without any major gaps among the various groups. These very same gaps, however, are used by evolutionists to classify living forms, distinguishing among family groups, classes, species, etc. The inconsistency of the presence of complicated invertebrates in the Cambrian level is summarized by J. Kerby Anderson and Harold G. Coffin:

"We have also seen that those invertebrates that first appear in the Cambrian period have been complex invertebrates. In no way can these early multicellular organisms be considered primitive. The later appearance of other invertebrates, groups such as the ammonites and insects, also do not give us any support for the various models of evolution. In summary, we should note that the explosion of life in the Cambrian period and the systematic gaps between major invertebrate 'kinds' are much more supportive evidence for the creation model than for the various models of evolution."[6]

91

The oldest fossil-bearing strata are those of the Cambrian period. In those strata, fossil remains of highly developed life forms have been found (corals, sponges, worms, crustacea, etc.). Highly developed representatives of several main classifications, even of animal classes, have been found in the Cambrian layer without any trace of common or more simple ancestors. Evolutionists postulate that these highly developed life forms required millions of years to evolve. Yet not a single authenticated multicellular fossil has been found in any strata earlier than the Cambrian. Even the traces of single cell organisms found in earlier strata are disputed. Even if the single cell fossils are confirmed, the empty gap between them and the incredibly varied and highly developed life forms from the Cambrian period cannot be

Evolutionists postulate that coal beds were formed by the sinking and rising of ground on which successive peat bogs developed. The vegetation from the peat bogs is said to have provided the material for the coal.

surmounted. This would mean that as much as nine-tenths of the history of earthly life has left no record.

Not a single proof in the fossil record supports the assumption that the single and multiple cell organisms are related in their germinal origins, or that all subsequent life forms are developed from earlier, more simple life forms. The theory of evolution is not documented by the fossil record. On the contrary, the oldest documentation we have shows that the main classifications of life forms existed side by side from the beginning. Rather than picturing the history of life as a gigantic family tree, we instead can picture it as a large graph of more or less closely associated bars, representing the history of major classes as separate from the beginning. Davidheiser summarizes, responding to explanations for the lack of evolutionary support in the Cambrian fossil record:

"Although it is claimed that there is some evidence of life before that assigned to the time called the Cambrian Period, the fossil record begins there with a great abundance of fossils. This has to be explained, and a number of theories have been suggested. The two most commonly presented are: (1) the older rocks have been transformed by heat and pressure so that the fossils they contained were destroyed (but there are rocks of this alleged age which are not so transformed and which are suitable for containing fossils, but have none), (2) the creatures which lived at that time were too soft to leave fossils (but there are many fossil jellyfish, and what is softer than a jellyfish, and why would soft things get hard shells so suddenly?)"[7]

Even in Darwin's day the lack of early evolutionary life-form fossils was a problem for evolutionists. Darwin hoped that further field work would uncover the missing confirmations:

"If the theory of evolution is correct, the Cambrian fauna should be preceded by a series of increasingly complex ancestors. In Charles Darwin's day, paleontology was a young science. It was his belief that continued search for fossils would reveal the ancestors to the amazing array of intricate Cambrian animals."[8]

Cambrian fossil beds represent most classes of the animal kingdom.
Right: A fossilized dragonfly, wings outstretched.
Below: Fossilized snails (Turritella).

We conclude from the evidence (only briefly touched on above) that the Cambrian strata, if they represent the earliest strata formed with fossils from living organisms, provide no support to the evolutionary model that complex forms developed from more simple life forms over an extremely long period of time. Gish provides a summary of the record:

"From all appearances, then, based on the known facts of the historical record, there occurred a great burst of life at a high level of complexity. The fossil record gives no evidence that these Cambrian animals were derived from preceding ancestral forms. Furthermore, not a single fossil has been found that can be considered to be a transitional form between the major groups, or phyla. At their earliest appearance, these major invertebrate types were just as clearly and distinctly set apart as they are today. Thus, trilobites have always been trilobites, brachiopods have always been brachiopods, corals have always been corals, jellyfish have always been jellyfish, etc., and the fossil record offers no indication whatsoever that these highly varied invertebrate types have been derived from common ancestors."[9]

Transitional Forms in the Fossil Record

Evolutionists are quick to point out that many orders and families of the animal kingdom are not represented in the Cambrian strata but

appear only in more recent strata. This is used as evidence that those recent life forms developed or evolved from the earlier life forms so abundant in the Cambrian age.

Part of the creationist answer to the above is to question the evolutionists' methods of dating the different strata. We will discuss this at length later. For now we will merely say that without exception the animal and plant families, orders, and classes appear suddenly in "more recent" strata, without any intermediate forms. If they did develop from the Cambrian life forms, where are the transition fossils?

Above: A fossilized herring, its remains showing no decomposition.
Right: A beautiful spotted salamander (Salamandra salamandra terrestris) and its larval stage (far right). The salamander is an amphibian. Evolutionists believe that amphibians evolved twice over several million years.
Below: A fossilized ray, related to the shark, showing its specialized electrical system.

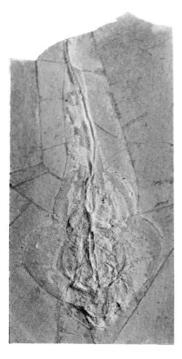

When fossil "proofs" for general evolution are presented, it is usually within the vertebrate classification since the fish, amphibians, reptiles, birds, and mammals seem to appear in successive strata. Each of those classes, however, in their various orders, always appears suddenly in the fossil record, without intermediate forms. There are four classes of fish: the jawless, the placoderms (armored fish, now extinct), the cartilaginous fish, and the bony fish. The first two groups, which are alleged to be the ancestors of modern fish, contain several orders that are very different from one another and for which no common ancestors have been found among the fossils. The placoderms appear in strata where we would expect, according to the evolution model, to find the ancestors of the cartilaginous and bony fish. However, the placoderms themselves are a widely varied group with their own species, and any derivation of the higher fish from the placoderms is anatomically impossible. Then, too, the cartilaginous and bony fish appear suddenly, with no transitionary forms in the fossil record.

According to evolutionists, the amphibians evolved from the fish, a process that must have taken millions of years and a tremendously large number of transitional forms to accomplish such a great transformation through minute adaptive and mutational changes. Several groups of fossil fish have been suggested as providing the transitional forms

94

that led to amphibians. But not a single fossil has been found that can be authenticated as a transitional form between any of those fish and any amphibian fossil. Instead, we find that the various amphibian orders appear simultaneously, with marked differences among them and no known common ancestors.

The lineage of amphibians becomes more confused when we discover that during the Mesozoic age (we will dispute evolutionary dating by rock strata later) there are no fossil amphibians at all. Between the various extinct amphibians of the Paleozoic age and the three living sub-classes of amphibians today, no fossil link exists. We propose that

A giant Galapagos Island turtle (Geochelone elephantopus). Reptiles are said to have evolved from amphibians.

the dating system of the evolutionists is completely unreliable, and that the various forms of amphibians developed relatively quickly from the original amphibious prototypes, created by God.

Gish has an interesting discussion of the "fish to amphibian" hypothesis:

"For a long time it was assumed that the fish that evolutionists believe gave rise to the amphibians became extinct about 70 million years ago. In rocks which evolutionists assume are 70 million years or younger, no fossils of the fish have ever been found. In about 1939, however, this type of fish was found to be alive and well off the coast of Africa. It is a cross-opterygian fish of the genus *Latimeria*. It was taken from a depth of about 5,000 feet. Here he is still very much the same fish that is supposed to have given rise to the amphibians multiplied millions of years ago. It would certainly be astounding to believe that he has remained so genetically and morphologically stable for all those millions of years while his cousin was evolving all the way to man! Furthermore, how could *any* creature be on this earth for 70 million years without leaving a trace in the fossil record? Perhaps there is something wrong with evolutionary assumptions!"[10]

Evolutionists have fewer problems asserting their belief that amphibians evolved into reptiles. This is not because there exists clear fossil evidence of such an evolution, but because amphibian and reptilian skeletal structures are so similar. The major differences between amphibians and reptiles are in their soft parts, which are generally not fossilized. The evolutionists have the comparatively simple task of finding similar fossil skeletal parts and proclaiming them related or transitionary forms. That, however, offers no concrete evidence of evolution or transition forms at all. Anderson and Coffin discuss this problem:

"If amphibians evolved into reptiles, the fossil record should provide documentation for this important event. *Seymouria* has been suggested as one possible transitional form....*Seymouria* is a small tetrapod found in the upper portion of the lower Permian sediments exposed to the north of the town of Seymour, Texas. The major difficulty with *Seymouria* is that the period in which it is found is too late in the rock period to be the grandparent of the reptiles. It is found in the Permian period, while reptiles such as Hylonomus...are found as early as the Pennsylvanian period. Thus, we have a situation in which the children are older than the grandparents. Further investigation has shown that *Seymouria* probably had an aquatic amphibian life history and should be classified with the amphibians.

"*Seymouria* was selected as a transitional form because of the number of reptilian skeletal features it possessed. Unfortunately, skeletal features are not always a good indication of an organism's relationship with other organisms. Modern amphibians can easily be distinguished from modern reptiles by means of their external soft parts. The fossil record, however, does not preserve soft parts, thus it is often impossible to make a clear distinction. Furthermore, reptiles differ from amphibians in that reptiles lay an amniotic egg. Although this is a good diagnostic feature, it is not preserved with any regularity in the fossil record. In summary, it should be noted that our difficulty in classifying certain fossil finds of amphibians and reptiles is not a result of a close affinity between the groups, but it is rather a result of a fossil record that cannot give us all of the facts we need to make an objective decision."[11]

The Origin of Warm-blooded Animals

The warm-blooded animals are the only ones able to maintain a stable, relatively high body temperature. The origin of warm-bloodedness is one problem with which evolutionists are unable to cope by the use of fossil evidence. Mammals are also skeletally similar to the reptiles, but their soft parts are very different (hair, skin, mammary glands for the nursing of young, etc.).

The two most striking differences between the skeletal parts of mammals and reptiles are ears and jaws. All mammals (both fossil and living) have a single lower jawbone. All reptiles (fossil or living) have at least four bones on either side of the lower jaw. All mammals have three middle ear bones on each side. All reptiles have only one ear bone on each side. Not a single fossil exists with transitionary forms of jaws and/or ears. But evolution tells us that the transitionary forms must have existed. (Perhaps two of the lower jaw bones of some reptiles moved to their ears!) If evolutionists insist on a gradual transition, then how did the transitional forms chew with lower jaws that were not properly hinged, or how could they hear during the complete re-organization of the bones in their ears?

Above: Cormorants in Kenya. Below: A cuckoo-like bird from Africa, which has claws on its wings. Such claws are not characteristic of birds.

The evolution from reptiles to birds is also an enigma, despite the fact that evolutionists believe they can produce the fossil of a true transitionary form, *Archaeopteryx*. However, *Archaeopteryx* is fully a bird, not a birdlike reptile. The development of a flying animal requires changes in virtually every structure of the nonflying ancestor. We would expect to find numerous transitional forms in a process that requires so many changes. When we consider that this must have taken place at least four times in the evolutionary process (insects, flying reptiles, birds, and bats), then the fossil remnants should be especially numerous. But no transitional series have been found leading to any of the four flying animal types we have today. All four kinds of flying animals appear suddenly in the fossil record, complete, and frequently

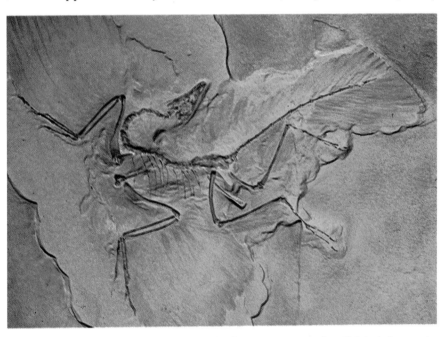

Fossilized Archaeopteryx, *said by evolutionists to be a transitionary form between reptiles and birds.*

in varying forms. Nevertheless, *Archaeopteryx*, a fossil bird from the Jurassic strata, is presented as the closest thing to a transitional form evolutionists have found yet. However, as Gish remarked, the *Archaeopteryx* was no true transitional form:

"Thus, in not a single instance concerning the origin of flight can a transitional series be documented, and in only one case has a single intermediate form been alleged. In the latter case, the so-called intermediate is no real intermediate at all because, as paleontologists acknowledge, *Archaeopteryx* was a true bird—it had wings, it was completely feathered, it *flew*.... It was not a half-way bird, it *was* a bird."[12]

The so-called reptile features of the *Archaeopteryx* fossils consist of clawlike appendages on the edges of the wings, teeth, vertebrae that are turned outward along the tail, and a small breastbone. However, those characteristics do not prove that *Archaeopteryx* is a transitionary form between reptiles and birds, since some birds living today possess similar traits. Anderson and Coffin discuss this similarity:

"First, it should be noted that some of its characteristics that are considered reptilian can also be found in other living and extinct birds. For example, *Archaeopteryx* had claws on its wings. However, many other birds have claws on their wings as well. Many birds have a claw on the first digit (finger) and gallinaceous birds (grouse, turkey, chicken), birds of prey, waders, and swimming birds have a claw on the second digit in the embryo and occasionally in the adult. Many ratites, such as the rhea *(Rhea)* and the ostrich *(Struthio)*, possess claws on the first, second, and third digits.

"There is also a bird found in South America known as the hoatzin *(Opisthocomus hoazin)*, which possesses strong claws on its first and second digits and has rudimentary claws on its third and fourth digits. Thus, it would be considered more primitive than *Archaeopteryx* because of its claws and other anatomical features.

"Another feature of *Archaeopteryx* that is considered reptilian is its

The duck-billed platypus, with a tail like a beaver, poison-filled spurs on his hind legs, otter-like webbed feet, a bill like a duck, and mammary glands.

teeth. Modern birds do not possess teeth, but we know that some extinct birds had teeth. Reptiles of that period had a wide variety of dentition, while most modern reptiles do not have true teeth. The teeth of *Archaeopteryx* do not fit nicely into any scheme of progressive evolution, and they do not seem to be good candidates for transitional structures....

"The most important diagnostic features of *Archaeopteryx* are those that are avian. *Archaeopteryx* is considered to be a bird because it has feathers and wings. These feather impressions are not primitive feathers, nor are they transitional structures between scales and wings, but they are modern feathers in every respect. The presence of feathers also implies that *Archaeopteryx* possessed the internal physiology (a warm-blooded circulation) and biochemistry (an endocrine system for molting of feathers) that are generally associated with modern birds. The presence of wings with feathers is sufficient to classify it with all modern birds."[13]

Evolution Among Mammals

We have surveyed a few of the indications that plant and animal life was created in several groups or "kinds," from which limited adaptation and development occurred. We reject the macroevolution model. When we look at the lack of evidence for the evolution of orders within the class of mammals, we come to the same conclusion.

Consider the order of the bats, who, like the insects, flying reptiles, and birds, are capable of flying, albeit in a very different manner. Bats are said by evolutionists to have developed from the insectivores (which include moles, shrews, etc.). It should be obvious that major changes must occur necessarily for a molelike animal to become a flying bat. The "hands" of the insectivore would have to grow enormously, since the flying web of the bat is stretched between the four elongated "fingers" and the hind legs. Fossil bats have been found, some in the lower reaches of the Tertiary strata. But again, even the oldest bats are still bats. Anderson and Coffin discuss the lack of evolutionary evidence for the bat:

Right: A living bat, which is identical to the fossilized bat on the next page.
Below: A member of the insectivore class, from which evolutionists postulate bats evolved.

"The last group of animals with the capacity of flight was the mammals. Of the mammals, only the bats successfully developed flight. The earliest fossil evidence of flying bats 'is in fully developed bats of the Eocene epoch.' This first bat is *Icaronycteris index.* By comparing it with a modern brown bat *Myotis myotis,* we can see that it is quite well developed.... If bats evolved from shrewlike ancestors, there is certainly no fossil evidence to support it. *Icaronycteris* is a very advanced flying mammal. Glenn Jepsen of Princeton University has stated that this Eocene bat 'is not a "missing link" between shrews or anything else and bats, but already a true bat.'"[14]

The Evolution and Classification of Different Mammals

The various rodent families appear in the fossil record without any transitional forms. The evolutionary scheme has no explanation for the origin of beavers, old world porcupines, and others. Hares and rabbits used to be considered a suborder of the rodents, but today are considered a separate order. They are so intrinsically different that they cannot be classified with any other mammalian order. Even the oldest fossils of these animals exhibit all of the unique characteristics of the contemporary order.

This type of problem concerns the classification of man, too. Biologists consider man a part of the primate order, which includes shrews, lemurs, tarsiers, monkeys, apes, and man. The evolutionists picture the primates as having developed from an order of insectivores. However, they have been unable to trace the true origin of the lower primates (shrews, lemurs, and tarsiers). The fossil record has no transitional forms; existing fossils of the lower primates are almost identical in form to living animals today. Any indication of transition from lower primates to other monkeys or the apes is absent.

Insects, Plants, and the Evolution Model

The fossil record concerning plants and insects also cannot support the evolution model. But it is consistent with the creation model, which

Right: A fossil of the oldest known bats from the Eiocene period. Even the flying web can be seen.
Below: The fossil record does not present a "family tree" for mammalian orders such as the apes.

states that God created all of the major life forms. which then reproduced and adapted "after their kinds."

Insects appear from the Devonian strata on in an overwhelming variety of forms and in enormous numbers. Two things stand out about the consistency of the fossil record concerning insects: (1) the insects appear on the scene suddenly, and there is no fossil evidence connecting them to any hypothetical ancestors; and (2) the fossil insects look almost exactly like contemporary living insects (although some varieties are much larger than contemporary insects). All the main orders of insects are found in fossils from the remains of the Oligocene forests.

Plants conform to that pattern as well. All main classifications seen today can be found in fossil strata from the Triassic on. Only the angiosperms do not appear until the Cretaceous age, but even then with no convincing fossil link to an evolutionary ancestor. There are numerous examples of plants (and insects) which changed little or not at all throughout the geologic ages. We refer the reader to the recommended reading list for further information.

Dating the Strata

As promised earlier in this chapter, we will discuss here the dating methods by which evolutionists determine the relative ages of the different strata in which fossils are found. Although many textbooks assume that strata dating is absolutely certain, such is not the case. Morris summarizes the illogical circular dating system of the fossil strata:

"The evolutionary interpretation of the fossil record is based on the assumption that the simpler fossils are found in older rocks. However, it is also true that rocks are dated primarily by the fossils they contain.

"The main proof of evolution (the fossil sequence) is derived from the relative age of the rocks, which is determined on the basis of the assumed evolutionary sequence of the fossils. *One can prove*

Large numbers of plants appear in the Carboniferous strata, often of group types which appear suddenly in the fossil record.
Right: Mariopteris *appear in large numbers, as do the coral* Lonsdaleia *(far right).*

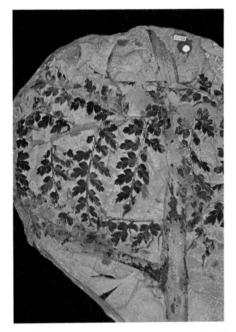

ANYTHING if he starts with his conclusion and then reasons in a circle."[15]

The circular illogical reasoning of the dating system evolutionists use with the fossil evidence is only part of their faulty chronology. Thurman has a helpful discussion of the dating problem:

"Evolutionists use several methods of dating fossils, all based on untestable assumptions. The most widely used method is based on the decay rate of several kinds of radioactive materials, such as the uranium-lead or potassium-argon 'atomic clocks.' An age is estimated by measuring the amount of uranium remaining in a rock sample, comparing it to the amount of lead formed and multiplying this by the decay rate.

"This method of dating fossils assumes several things, including: (1) only the radioactive material, and not any intermediate or final decay products (for example, lead) were initially present; (2) no intermediate or final product was added or lost since its initial formation (although some intermediate products are gases); and (3) the rate of radioactive decay has not varied since the beginning of time. Actually, what the scientists determine is only the amount of initial and decay products remaining in the sample. Determining the age requires calculations based on the above assumptions. If these assumptions are true, the calculated age is realistic. But until these assumptions can be supported, no dates based upon them can be known with certainty. There is some

101

A contemporary Latimeria, *discovered alive in the 1930s but also identified as a coelacanth, an order which was thought to have been extinct for hundreds of millions of years.*

question as to just how far the present can be extended into the past, especially when billions of years are involved."[16]

Conclusion

Our survey of the fossil record has been necessarily brief and selective. We have seen consistently, however, that the objective record does not support the evolution model. Instead, the record is consistent with the creation model. If the general theory of evolution was true, the fossil record would almost certainly provide abundant confirmation, or at the least it would not testify to the inconsistencies of the system. However, we find that the fossil record lacks any significant objective verification of evolution and does point to inconsistencies in evolutionary theory. Anderson and Coffin provide a good conclusion to this review:

"A theory based too largely on the hopes of future discoveries is not well grounded. If we take the fossil record at face value, if we accept the sudden appearance of complex forms, if we accept the discontinuities between major groups as a valid representation of the past history of life, we are led toward the belief that the major types of plants and animals are the products of sudden creation in the past."[17]

We are convinced that no fact in science, including the objective evidence of fossils, will ever controvert the biblical account. Morris

expresses such sentiments well, providing a good bridge to our discussion in chapters eight and nine concerning natural disasters, the design of God, and the great flood of Noah.

"The great fossil graveyards of land vertebrates — reptiles and mammals — are recognized in terms of Biblical geology to be herds of pre-diluvian animals which were overtaken by the vast sediments propelled by the Flood waters and buried before they could escape. In some of these cases, there may also be the possibility of burial by some post-Flood regional catastrophe. Great volcanic lava flows, earth movements, violent windstorms, and other catastrophes, including the great Ice Age, were after effects of the Flood, resulting from the global cataclysmic changes in the earth's lithosphere, hydrosphere, and atmosphere during the Flood."[18]

Above: A beautifully preserved insect fossil.
Below: One of the many kinds of trilobites, arthropods whose fossils are from the Paleozoic period.

CHAPTER SEVEN

What Is Man?

People around the world differ markedly according to size, skin, hair, bulk, and even cultural and social conventions. And yet, all human beings are of one species and are essentially the same. In the animal world, species differ from one to another in remarkable ways. The same God created all, man and animal, in His divine design.

To summarize our study thus far, we have discussed the development and role of science and faith; we have established that the universe exists and that it was created from or by something or Someone outside itself; we noted the design and order in the universe as consistent with the idea of a Creator like the God of the Bible; we observed that because of natural laws (the first and second laws of thermodynamics) life could not have begun spontaneously and therefore must have been created; we surveyed the history and general theory of evolution and concluded that the creation model makes more sense than the evolution model; and we saw the creation model affirmed by the testimony of the fossil record. In this chapter we will focus specifically on mankind.

What are human beings? How are we like and different from animals? Are we a special creation of God, or did we evolve from lower life or animal forms? Our discussion of this topic will be longer than any previous chapter, but still will cover just a small portion of the data available from science and the Bible.

"Then God said, 'Let the earth bring forth living creatures after their kind: cattle and creeping things and beasts of the earth after their kind'; and it was so. And God made the beasts of the earth after their kind, and the cattle after their kind, and every thing that creeps on the ground

An interesting perception of Adam and Eve, giving pictorial form to the consequences of their sin and to its effect on their descendents.

after its kind; and God saw that it was good. Then God said, 'Let Us make man in Our image, according to Our likeness; and let them rule over the fish of the sea and over the birds of the sky and over the cattle and over all the earth, and over every creeping thing that creeps on the earth.' And God created man in His own image, in the image of God He created him; male and female He created them. And God blessed them; and God said to them, 'Be fruitful and multiply, and fill the earth, and subdue it; and rule over the fish of the sea and over the birds of the sky, and over every living thing that moves on the earth.' Then God said, 'Behold, I have given you every plant yielding seed that is on the surface of all the earth, and every tree which has fruit yielding seed; it shall be food for you; and to every beast of the earth and to every bird of the sky and to everything that moves on the earth which has life, I have given every green plant for food'; and it was so. And God saw all that He had made and behold, it was very good. And there was evening and there was morning, the sixth day" (Genesis 1:24-31).

The above passage from Genesis 1 reminds us that mankind was the last and most significant creation by God during the creative period.

To begin, let us again note that the Bible does not specifically date the origin of the universe, the earth, life, or mankind. A. E. Wilder-Smith

106

summarizes the following concerning the biblical dating of creation:

"In view of the fact, therefore, that some genealogies and time charts are specifically very complete, it is remarkable that the important genealogy of Genesis 11 does not profess to be complete and does not sum up the total number of years elapsed from the start to finish. It looks as if Moses knew that his table was incomplete and that he therefore deliberately avoided his usual custom of totalling the years.... An excellent expose of this question of the incompleteness of the genealogies in the Old Testament was published nearly eighty years ago by the Rev. Professor William Henry Green of Princeton Theological Seminary....

"It is sufficient for our purposes here to point out that the Bible does not teach from its genealogies that the creation took place in the year 4004 B.C. Much longer time spans are legitimately allowable on the basis of the biblical world view and genealogies."[1]

By acknowledging the inexact dating of the early chapters of Genesis, we are not saying that we deny in any way that God is the sovereign Creator and that creation took place exactly as Genesis describes it. However, we are acknowledging that Genesis does not strictly limit the date or duration of creation.

Self-cognizant and self-actuating personhood will forever distinguish humans from machines, even sophisticated "thinking" computers.

"God created man (male and female) by an act of fiat creation (Genesis 1:27). The Bible allows no room for any theory of either organic or theistic evolution so far as the creation of man is concerned. Adam was created first, and immediately started to name the animals God had already created as God brought them before him. He looked for the fellowship of an I-thou relationship, similar to that which he already enjoyed with God from the beginning, but could not find it among the lower forms of creation (Genesis 2:20). Then, and only then, did God create Eve as his helpmeet (2:21-22)....

"Few if any scholars now feel that Ussher's chronology gives a satisfactory answer (creation in 4004 B.C.). It is quite commonly accepted by evangelicals that many of the names mentioned in the OT genealogical tables stand for leading genealogical names, and that the lists cover much longer periods of time (and often cover hundreds of years) than at first thought."[2]

Man was created in the image of God. In Genesis 2:7 we find more detail about the creation of man: "Then the Lord God formed man of dust from the ground, and breathed into his nostrils the breath of life; and man became a living being." Man's physical makeup was nothing new in God's creation. The first man was of the same material substance as the rest of the mammals. Modern biochemistry bears this out. We do not know what this first man looked like. His physical appearance is unimportant to us for two reasons. One, he evidently had the genetic potential to produce all of the varied human races we have in the world today (and through history), and so to picture him as a white European type is a baseless conjecture. Two, what was important about this first man, Adam, was that he was the only earthly creature that was *personal* (we will discuss personhood later in this chapter). Russell Mixter notes the unimportance of Adam's physical appearance as it relates to some questionable archaeological finds:

"Neither need the creationist have any quarrel with morphological

features of ancient man. The Bible, which is the creationist's basis of belief and life, simply says nothing about what Adam looked like. And, although the creationist, Protestant and Catholic alike, must of necessity hold to the belief... that there was a 'first man,' it is of no consequence whether he looked like a Pithecanthropoid or a Caucasoid. Furthermore, if anthropological opinion swings in favor of calling some prehistoric types by separate specific or generic names, and calls other types *Homo sapiens* with modern man, this is of relatively little consequence. For the creationist recognizes the arbitrary and non-qualitative nature of taxonomic categories and is not bound to equate any of them with the 'kind' spoken of in Genesis 1."[3]

Above: Brazilian Indians. Below: A native of West Irian (a province of Indonesia). Right: Caravaggio's Jesus at Emmaus. Even in diversity, mankind— in whatever time period and at whatver location around the globe— has exhibited the "image of God." Every human society ever recorded has included some kind of religious belief and practice.

The Image of God

The first human was very different from the rest of the life forms on the earth. Man was a spiritual being, created in the image of God: God breathed his breath of life into man's nostrils. Man possesses a spirit given by God (Ecclesiastes 12:7) and, in that respect, man is an entirely new creation, the high point of God's creative work. The entire earth with its various life forms was made subject to him. Man resembles God in that which separates him from the animals: His spiritual and moral attributes give him the capacity for communion and fellowship with God. After God created Adam, he created Eve, the first female human being.[4] They are referred to together in Genesis 1:27 ("male and female He created them"). Often we find the biblical translator using the word *man* or *mankind* to refer to both men and women. Those first two humans were the only part of God's earthly creation capable of worship. Only they possessed a spiritual nature. Henry Morris describes this special human attribute:

"The uniqueness of man lies not in his physiology, which has many similarities to that of the animals, nor even in his conscious intelligence, which is shared at least to some extent with the animals, but in his spiritual nature, the implanted 'image of God,' his capacity for abstract

108

thought, his awareness of esthetic and ethical values and, above all, his capacity for personal fellowship with his Creator."[5]

Even secular people see distinctions between humans and the rest of earthly life. While some materialists deny any qualitative difference between human beings and other life forms, most people, even if they are not religious, cannot ignore the special *qualitative* differences between themselves and animals. Old Testament scholar R. Laird Harris notes:

"Even from the secular point of view there is something special about man. There is an obvious similarity between horses and cows, between

All human societies, contemporary and historical, have incorporated religious belief and practice.
Above: Proper costuming is often significant for religious ritual.
Far Right: Stonehenge had special religious (astrological) significance.
Below: The Mayan god of the wind, Quetzalcoatle.

apes and monkeys. There is just as obvious a difference between apes and men. Similarities exist between men and the animal world. But no animal thinks as men do, communicates as men do, associates with like animals as men do, or rises to such heights and sinks to such depths as men do. Mankind differs from animals in physique, culture, mentality, and conduct in obvious ways. Are we then merely blood brother to the brute? It is not obvious that we are."[6]

What does it mean when we say that God created man *in his image*? We have seen some of the ways in which we reflect the nature of our Creator in a way no animal or plant ever does or can. God is a spiritual, moral, and rational being, and human beings, made in his image, are also spiritual, moral, and rational.

Differences Between Man and Animals

Man is different from all other animals in a number of ways, both immaterially and physically. We will review just a few of those differences below.

1. Man can *think analytically;* he can reason and philosophize. Along these lines, a non-Christian writer, Julian Huxley, noted that only man possesses true language and conceptual thought, art, humor, science,

and religion.[7]

2. Another distinction, also noted by Huxley, is that man can *record and make history;* he produces and appreciates culture.

3. Man can communicate by abstract symbols. He possesses *language* capability. One of the first responsibilities given Adam by God was to name the animals (Genesis 2:19-23).

4. Man is a *social being,* capable of conscious interaction and fellowship. Adam and Eve's union was much more significant than the mating of two animals. It was a spiritual and social union, a marriage, of which no animal is ever capable (Genesis 2:24).

An artist's concept of Neanderthal man, whose ancient societies included religion. Evolutionists admit that Neanderthal man does not represent "the missing link" in the evolutionary chain of mankind.

5. Man is an *economic being,* able to transact complicated business and to administer goods and services under his control. God instructed Adam and Eve to take control over the earth and "subdue" it (Genesis 1:28).

6. Man is an *aesthetic being,* capable of perceiving and appreciating beauty and intangible values. This is closely related to this *ethical* orientation (below).

7. Only man has an understanding of *justice,* more than just a simple awareness of right and wrong (which might be trained into a household pet with a few obedience lessons). Man understands and applies concepts of judgment and punishment in his societies.

8. Man is an *ethical being.* He can distinguish between good and bad, right and wrong. He can and does make moral judgments. He has a conscience. Only to man of all the animals could God talk of "good"

and "evil." Because of man's sense of justice and this ethical orientation, God could fairly punish him for his willful disobedience in the Garden of Eden.

9. Only man can experience *faith*. Man alone of all earthly creation can worship his Creator. Man alone can put his trust in the guidance and leadership of God. Harris notes:

"With such a God the Old Testament man is in constant confrontation. Man is thus regularly assumed to be a spiritual being. God's control extends to the animals, trees, clouds, storms, stars, and all else. But men are in fellowship with Him or they are trapped in their sin.

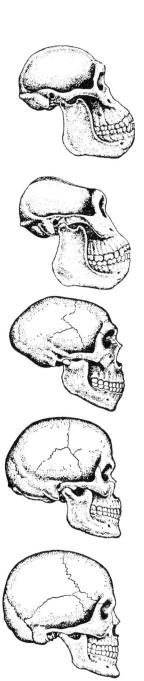

Above: Skull reconstructions made from various ancient skull fragments, in order from top to bottom: Australopithecus, Paranthropus, Neanderthal, Cromagnon, and Homo sapiens (modern man).
Right: An imaginative recreation of what Pithecanthropus might have looked like.
Far right: Remains of Pithecanthropus erectus, discovered by Dubois in 1891.

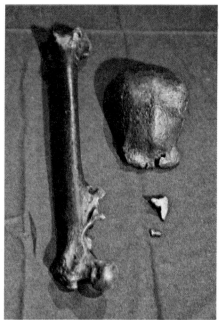

Man's relation to God is unique in all the world. God is the Father of those who have put their faith in Him. Believers are God's children. Israel is 'a people near unto him' (Ps. 148:14). 'Doubtless thou art our father' cries Isaiah (63:16). God's covenants with men are established from Adam and Noah on to the times of Ezekiel and Malachi. Man in the Old Testament is clearly pictured as having a spiritual nature and as being fully responsible to the one true living God whom he must worship and whom he must obey."[8]

As an aside, there are also significant ways in which we humans are different physiologically (materially) from animals. Some of our unique physical characteristics and/or abilities are listed by evolutionist Ashley Montagu:

"Fully erect posture, Bipedal locomotion, Legs much longer than arms, Comparatively vertical face, Great reduction in projection of jaws, Great reduction of canine teeth, Absence of a bony diastema in upper jaw for the reception of the tip of the canine tooth, Prominent nose with elongated tip (i.e., elongated beyond the nasal bone), Outward rolled mucous membrane of lips, A well marked chin, A forward lumbar convexity or curve, and Nonopposable great toes, set in line with other toes."[9]

Human Fossils and Evolution

We have surveyed briefly a general biblical anthropology and seen that human beings are the direct and special creation of God. But what is evolution's side of the picture? Does the fossil record concerning humankind support the idea that *Homo sapiens* developed from lower life forms and is merely a sophisticated animal? Although our survey of the fossils and of human evolution is necessarily brief, we are convinced that the evidence does not support the general theory of evolution but instead is consistent with a biblical anthropology.

As a preliminary note, it should be remembered that the fossil record

Dr. Duane Gish, prominent spokesman of the scientific creationist viewpoint, who believes all hominoid fossils are either ape or ape-type, or distinctly human. He does not accept that man evolved from less complex forms of life.

concerning mankind is scanty and what fossils do exist are most often fragmentary. We do not possess either the wealth or quality of fossils of humans and manlike animals that we do of other life forms. Some argue that humans and other primates mostly lived near the equator, and the humid tropical climates were not conducive to fossil preservation. We do, however, possess human and primate fossils from nontropical areas, and most evolutionists will agree that man or "protoman" lived in a variety of environments, including environments where abundant numbers of other life forms were preserved as fossils. Klotz notes the significant problem with the fragmentary nature of most primate or human fossils:

"Another striking thing is the fragmentary character of most of these fossils. There are few complete skulls and even fewer complete skeletons. Often the entire find is represented by a piece of the skull or by a jawbone. Certainly any reconstruction based upon such fragmentary remains is extremely precarious. Hooton calls attention to this by saying that when we recall the fragmentary condition of most of these fossil skulls and when we remember that the faces are usually missing, we can readily see that even the reconstruction of the facial *skeletons* [italics his] leaves room for a great deal of doubt as to details. To attempt to reconstruct the soft parts, he points out, is an even more hazardous undertaking. The lips, the eyes, the ears and the nasal tip leave no clues on the underlying bony parts. Hooton says that you can model on a Neanderthal skull either the features of a chimpanzee or those of a philosopher. He concludes by saying that the alleged restorations of ancient types of man have very little, if any scientific value and are likely only to mislead the public."[10]

Another problem we have with the fossil record concerning human beings is even more serious than those already mentioned with typical fossil formations. Dating of any fossil remains, as we saw in the last two chapters, is at best a guess and at worst illogical and circular, of no practical use at all. When the subject is human or humanlike fossils, the problem is worse. That is because many human cultures bury their dead; ceremonial burial is one thing that has distinguished humans from other animals. Now, if an early man died during one time period, and his contemporaries buried him at any appreciable depth below the surface of the ground, it would be very easy for a scientist, finding the remains thousands of years later, to assume that the individual had lived in the stratum in which his remains were found. Of course, sometimes there are telltale clues to the burial and its depth, which will aid in adjusting the age of some fossil remains. But the clues are not always there and the chance of misdating a bone because of burial is real.

The stone commemorating the place where the Piltdown Man fragments were found (1912, 1913) by Charles Dawson. First heralded as "the missing link," the remains were later shown to be a hoax (see text).

When the general theory of evolution gained popularity after Darwin's works, evolutionists were eager to find the fossil remains that would provide the "missing links" in the evolutionary chain from primate ancestor to modern man. One of the first finds was made in 1890 by a Dutchman, Eugene Dubois, who led an expedition to Java to find man's ancestors in the fossil record. In 1891 he discovered the upper part of a skull and a few teeth in a riverbank. A year later, in 1892, he found a human femur (leg bone) only 15 meters from the original discovery. Those two finds became the first fossil "evidence" of the apelike ancestor of modern man. The human prototype was called, popularly, Java man (scientific name *Pithecanthropus erectus;* later *Homo erectus*). Had Dubois not associated the human femur with the teeth and skull portion, and had they not been of the same approximate age, most scientists would have classified it as a true ape, not a protohuman. What is perhaps most startling about Dubois's work is that for thirty years he hid two other skulls which were found near the same location and at approximately the same level. The two skulls were almost identical to modern aborigines! Gish comments on Dubois's omission and gives an opinion as to the reason for it:

"Dubois concealed the fact that he had also discovered at nearby Wadjak and at approximately the same level two human skulls (known as the Wadjak skulls) with a cranial capacity of about 1550-1650 c.c., somewhat above the present human average. To have revealed this fact at that time would have rendered it difficult, if not impossible, for his Java Man to have been accepted as a 'missing link.' It was not until 1922, when a similar discovery was about to be announced, that Dubois revealed the fact that he had possessed the Wadjak skulls for over 30 years. His failure to reveal this find to the scientific world at the same time he exhibited the *Pithecanthropus* bones can only be labeled as an act of dishonesty and calculated to obtain acceptance of *Pithecan-*

thropus as an ape-man."[11]

Although the present authors are not sure that Dubois was deliberately trying to be dishonest, his unethical concealment of the two human skulls shows the lengths to which some persons will go in an effort to document their own firm convictions to others.

Other scattered discoveries of human or humanlike fossils were found in the 1920s and 1930s and were eventually classified as part of the general class of *Homo erectus*. In 1921 two molars were found at a fossil dig near the village of Choukoutien in China. In 1927 another molar was found. Over the years of the dig a total of almost forty individuals

Right: Dr. John W. Cuozzo, orthodontist, whose extensive studies of contemporary jaws and dental structures led him to conclude that, because of the great variation, it would be almost impossible to tell the fossil orthodontic remains of apes from that of humans. Below: One artist's reconstruction of Leakey's Zinjanthropus.

 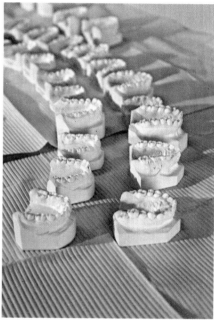

were said to be represented by the various tooth, skull, and bone fragments found. The fragments were found in a large fossil deposit of contemporaneous animals. Scientists surmised that the deposit represented the contents of a completely filled giant cavern. There were arguments over whether the cave was filled with a one time stratum of material (indicating a quick filling of the cavern) or with a multitude of strata (indicating an extremely slow filling of the cavern over perhaps thousands of years. However, regardless of how the cavern was filled or how long it took, all of the animal and supposed human fossil remains were closely related within their respective classifications and probably represented, given the evolution model, the same level of development.

The new fossil fragments were used to postulate a human ancestor that the scientists dubbed popularly, Peking man, or, more scientifically, *Sinanthropus*. There was debate about whether or not *Sinanthropus* should be classified as of approximately the same evolutionary stage as Java man *(Pithecanthropus)*, and therefore labeled *Pithecanthropus pekinensis*. The outcome of the debate was to classify both *Pithecanthropus* and *Sinanthropus* as representatives of *Homo erectus*. During World War II all of the fossils disappeared and have not been seen since. However, photographs and plaster casts had been made of the fossils and these continued to be studied by evolutionists. Of course,

The African Olduvai Gorge, where Louis and Mary Leakey spent years searching for fossil remains of man's evolutionary ancestors. Most of their finds are classified as Australopithecus.

lacking the actual fossils makes it absolutely impossible to use new dating to attempt to verify the fossils' ages.

What is most important to creationists in the *Sinanthropus* find is the manner or state in which the fossils were found. Since they were found with fossils of other game animals, the general consensus is that they, along with the other animals found, were the victims of primitive hunters. Gish comments:

"All authorities agree that every one of the *Sinanthropus* individuals had been killed by hunters and eaten. All of the skulls had been bashed in near the base in order that the brains might be extracted and eaten. Practically nothing of these creatures was found except fragments of the skull, and that in spite of the fact that fragments of almost 40 different individuals were recovered. The only question remaining unanswered in respect to these circumstances was, *who was the hunter*?"[12]

Evolutionists wonder if those primitive protomen practiced cannibalism or if *Sinanthropus* was victimized by some other primitive ancestor to man. Creationists wonder if the *Sinanthropus* fossils represent apes or nonhuman primates who were hunted and eaten by early, but fully human, men—or if the *Sinanthropus* fossils are the remains of an extinct but fully human race. Neither of those two creationist views

115

violates in any way the scientific evidence or the biblical account of the creation of man.

Famous Fossil Hoaxes and Mistakes

As we have said several times, the dating and identification of fossil remains are very difficult. Often the scientists must admit that their conclusions are just guesses, and often broad guesses. Among the humanlike fossil remains scientists have found are those that were later unequivocally shown to be frauds or misidentifications. We will mention some of them here. Sometimes those involved in the find or identification seemed to be aware of or even to have participated in

Australopithecus *skull (lower jaw, left; rest of skull, right) reconstructed from small fossil fragments.*

promoting fraud. At other times there were honest, if perhaps over-zealous, misdatings or misidentifications.

One mistake which can probably be attributed to overzealous misidentification concerns a molar found in Nebraska in 1922. It was identified as coming from an important transition form between man and his primate ancestors by at least four well-known scientists: H. Cook, H. F. Osborn, H. H. Wilder, and G. E. Smith. Osborn declared, on the day he first saw the tooth:

"The instant your package arrived I sat down with the tooth, in my window, and said to myself: 'It looks one hundred percent anthropoid' ...it looks to me as if the first anthropoid ape of America has been found."[13]

However, in 1927 the molar was correctly identified as that of a pig: "The men from the museum also found more of the fossil material for which they were looking, and it turned out that the tooth which had caused such a sensation was the tooth of an animal which had previously been named *Prosthennops*. This was very embarrassing, because *Prosthennops* was a peccary, which is a type of pig!"[14]

Perhaps the most famous humanoid fossil fraud was the Piltdown man, which fooled paleontologists for over forty years before it was proved that the skull was that of a modern man and the jawbone that of a modern ape. In the early 1900s two well-known British geologists, including Dr. Charles Dawson, were digging fossils at a quarry in the south of England. They claimed to have discovered a human skull next to an apelike jawbone. Their discovery became the famous Piltdown man. A second human skull was found in the same quarry later by Professor Sir Arthur Smith-Woodward, a seeming confirmation of the first find. Many anthropologists had been skeptical of the Dawson find, but the Smith-Woodward find convinced most of them that Piltdown

Right: 1959 photograph of Louis and Mary Leakey with skull fossil of Zinjanthropus.
Below: Plaque marking the discovery site of the Zinjanthropus *skull.*

man was a genuine example of the evolution of man from more primitive primates. Piltdown man (designated scientifically as *Eanthropus dawsoni*, or "Dawn Man") was said to be around 500,000 years old.

However, by 1950 sophisticated dating and chemical analysis techniques were applied to the Piltdown remains. The findings were startling. The skull was dated at just a few thousand years old, certainly that of a "modern" man. The jawbone was not fossilized at all and was only about as old as the year of its "discovery." It was definitely identified as the jawbone of a modern ape. Gish summarizes the investigation and its results:

"By 1950 a method had become available for assigning a relative age to fossil bones. This method is dependent on the amount of fluoride absorbed by bones from the soil. When the Piltdown bones were subjected to this test, it was discovered that the jawbone contained practically no fluoride and thus was no fossil at all. It was judged to be no older than about the year it was found. The skull did have a significant amount of fluoride, but was estimated to be a few thousand years old rather than 500,000 years old.

"With this information at hand, the bones were subjected to a thorough and critical examination. It was discovered that the bones had been treated with iron salts to make them look old, and scratch marks were detected on the teeth, indicating that they had been filed. In other words, Piltdown Man was a complete fraud! A modern ape's jaw and a human skull had been doctored to resemble an ape-man, and the forgery had succeeded in fooling most of the world's greatest experts. The success of this monumental hoax served to demonstrate that scientists, just like everyone else, are very prone to find what they are looking for whether it is there or not. The success of the Piltdown hoax for nearly 50 years in spite of the scrutiny of the world's greatest authorities, along with other stories nearly as dubious, led Lord Zuckerman to declare that it is doubtful if there is any science at all in the search for man's fossil ancestry."[15]

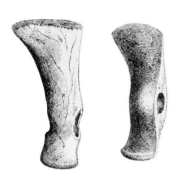

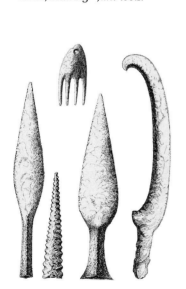

Above and Below: Drawings of various flint tools favored by ancient humans.
Right: A drawing of men "manufacturing" flint tools.

Piltdown man and the Nebraska pig's tooth are just two of the blunders or hoaxes that have been exposed in the search for man's fossil ancestors. While we cannot discount all finds, or even many finds, as hoaxes or misidentifications, we must learn a lesson from the frauds and misidentifications of the past. It is possible to be tricked or to make mistakes in identification and dating. Human fossil remains are few, fragmentary, and often found in the same vicinity as other animal fossil fragments. The chance of fossils being mixed up and misidentified is real and must be taken into account. Wilder-Smith echos our sentiments.

"Under no circumstances do we wish to create the impression that all the human fossil discoveries have been of the caliber of the Piltdown hoax. They have not. The point we wish to emphasize here is that it is easy, even today, to make huge errors where dating of ancient specimens is concerned, especially if one works too much on a theoretical background."[16]

Humanoid Fossils and Circular Dating Methods

Part of the problem in dating human and primate fossils is that scientists often use circular reasoning in ascertaining dates. If a fossil is judged to be "primitive," or more "apelike," then it is judged to be very

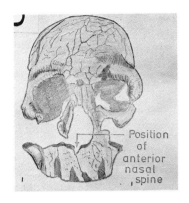

old. This is the same kind of problem we discussed in chapter six. Often rock strata are dated by the relative complexity or lack of complexity of fossil life found in them, and then the fossil life is dated by the stratum in which it is found. With the human fossil record the same problem occurs. Modern fossil remains are judged to be from very recent times. What happens when a modern skull is found in an undeniably old stratum (early Pleistocene or earlier)? The modern skull is rejected. Although the paleontologist may not know *how* the modern skull got into the old stratum, he is convinced that it must have happened by some accident. It could not be evidence that modern man existed during the time period represented by that stratum. It wouldn't

Above: The famous skull discovered in 1972 by Richard Leakey, estimated to be 2.9 million years old, but clearly human.
Right: Satirical painting parodying Michelangelo's painting of the creation of man. A smiling Darwin is overseeing the creation of a giant ape as man's ancestor.
Below: Richard Leakey, whose field research has continued and extended the work of his parents.

fit the evolutionary model.

In the following section we summarize the "evidence" for modern man's many anthropoid ancestors, as such evidence appears in the fossil record. We will see that there is no direct evidence that modern man ever evolved from essentially more primitive and qualitatively different primates.

Man's Family Tree

All of the anthropoid fossils that have not been discredited as frauds or misidentifications can be grouped under three main categories: (1) Neanderthal man, (2) Homo erectus, and (3) Australopithecus. Every fossil found so far can be identified characteristically with one of those three categories.

1. *Neanderthal man.* Many remains have been found of Neanderthal man. This, in fact, was the only fossil material available to Darwin when he wrote *The Descent of Man.* While Neanderthal man used to be described as stooped, wild, hairy, and not very intelligent, today he is classified as belonging to our own species, *Homo sapiens.* Davidheiser summarizes the importance of the later assessment of Neanderthal man's posture:

"After a thorough examination of the skeleton they concluded, 'He cannot, in view of his manifest pathology, be used to provide us with a reliable picture of a healthy, normal Neanderthalian. Notwithstanding, if he could be reincarnated and placed in a New York subway—provided he were bathed, shaved, and dressed in modern clothing—it is doubtful whether he would attract any more attention than some of its other denizens.' They affirm that 'there is thus no valid reason for the assumption that the posture of Neanderthal man...differed significantly from that of present-day men...there is nothing in this total morphological pattern to justify the common assumption that Neanderthal man was other than a fully erect biped when standing and walking.'"[17]

Evidently the first substantial Neanderthal skeleton was of a man who

suffered from arthritis and rickets. No wonder he appeared stooped!

"Straus reported, however, that after a recent re-examination of the original bones, there was abundant evidence of advanced osteoarthritis in the La Chapelle mandible and throughout the post-cranial skeleton. The vertebrae not only reveal marked 'lipping' and deformation, but indicate as well, significantly faulty repair on the part of the earlier investigators. He pointed out that recently Aramburg and Schultz have seriously questioned the 'naturalness of semi-erect posture in a habitually bipedal stance.' Furthermore, Aramburg has shown that modern man has frequently the same form of vertebrae as La Chapelle, proving that it was not a simian feature as Boule had thought."[18]

We conclude that Neanderthal man was no more different from modern man qualitatively than could be explained by differences such as racial characteristics we see today around the world. His proportionate brain size (percentage compared to body size) is within normal modern human parameters.

2. *Homo erectus.* Peking man and Java man (discussed above) are both classified as *Homo erectus*, which is thought to be a predecessor of *Homo sapiens* (modern man). It is now recognized, however, that some examples of *Homo erectus* seem to be more recent than some examples of *Homo sapiens.* Such a time overlap tends to discredit the idea that

120

Different ways humans have used art to depict the order and sovereignty apparent in the universe. The Egyptians had the sphinx (far left), the Greeks had Hercules (left), and the Christians had Jesus Christ (right, from Rembrandt). Only Jesus Christ is the way, the truth, and the life (John 14:6).

Homo erectus developed into *Homo sapiens.*

Anthropologist F. Weidenreich was of the opinion that all so-called *erectus* types should be classified as a subgroup of *Homo sapiens.* Such a classification would assume considerable variability within the species *sapiens.* Other scientists are of the opinion that some fossils classified as *erectus* should be identified more properly as true apes. Klotz notes Weidenreich's opinion:

"Weidenreich goes still further. He believes that the anatomical evidence offers no alternative but to unite all of the known human fossils and modern man in a single species, *Homo sapiens.* While he suggests that the South African forms may constitute a separate species not in the human line, *Pithecanthropus* and *Sinanthropus* are definitely included in *Homo sapiens.* Certainly this reduction to one species or even to one genus and three species, one of which is our modern *Homo sapiens,* is striking. Perhaps the problem of fossil men is not so troublesome a one after all."[19]

3. *Australopithecus.* Many different African finds, which originally had been given a wide variety of names, are now classified as *Australopithecus.* Especially rich finds have been made by the Leakey family in Tanzania. For thirty years Louis and Mary Leakey worked in the Olduvai Gorge in search of the fossil remains of transitional forms

between primitive apes and modern man. On the basis of their finds and other finds in Africa, *Australopithecus* had been divided into two categories: *Australopithecus robustus* and the lighter *Australopithecus habilis* (sometimes called *Australopithecus africanus*). A general description of this fossil form includes a skull capacity just a little larger than a modern gorilla's but quite a bit smaller than that of modern man. The jaw is shaped more like a human than an ape. The molars are massive and the jaw is very heavy. Most scientists agree that *Australopithecus* walked like other apes, with knuckles on the ground. Some believe *Australopithecus* is just that, an extinct form of ape, not directly related to human development at all. The tools found in the proximity of the *Australopithecus* fossils could have been used by some other human rather than by *Australopithecus*, who even could have been an ancient human prey.

The finds in 1974 by Donald Johanson ("Lucy" and her thirteen companions) are a subclass of *Australopithecus*. Although Johanson identifies them as the "missing links" between apes and humans, there is nothing in their appearance to distinguish them significantly from other *Australopithecus* finds. If we classify those as extinct apes instead of primitive humans, Johanson's finds present no problem to creationists. The only real connection between *Australopithecus* and man is the tools found in the vicinity of the fossils. The evolutionists assume, without evidence, that *Australopithecus* used the tools. Creationists are just as reasonable in assuming that the tools belonged to true humans who · hunted *Australopithecus*.

"Early in 1973, Richard Leakey gave a lecture in San Diego describing his latest results. He stated his convictions that these findings simply eliminate everything we have been taught about human origins and, he went on to say, he had nothing to offer in its place! Creationists *do* have something to offer in its place, of course. We believe that these results support man's special creation rather than his origin from an animal ancestry. These results also strongly support our belief that man and the ape have always coexisted."[20]

We conclude that man has been human from the beginning. We did not evolve from some other life form and we are not related in origin to any primate. We agree with the summary of Harris:

"To summarize our consideration of fossil man, we may say that new discoveries and further study have radically changed the picture. There is evidence for some variation within the human pattern, but the evidence that fossil men were even markedly different from today's man is questionable. Even the African finds do not show missing links but forms with human stature, human teeth, and as far as can be discerned, brain capacities within human ranges."[21]

Why do evolutionists continue to insist that human beings developed from more primitive life forms, and that humans and modern primates have common ancestors? They do not base their insistence on the evidence because, as we have seen in our brief survey, the evidence is sketchy at best and certainly open to divergent explanations. No, the evolution of humankind from lower life forms is necessary if one holds certain presuppositions that are diametrically opposed to Scripture. Many modern scientists are convinced absolutely that God does not

Moses and the Ten Commandments. It was Moses, writing under the inspiration of the Holy Spirit, who wrote of God's creative acts in Genesis 1-3.

exist, and that the universe we see around us is a product of mindless chance (see chapter two for a discussion of that theory). Many modern scientists are absolute materialists, that is, they believe that the material world is the only thing real. From this it follows logically that human beings are "machines," and human thoughts are only the product of chemical processes in the brain, developed by chance over the millennia. Scientists with such presuppositions *must*, therefore, defend the evolution of humankind from more simple life forms. With their theory all framed, and the details all filled in, such scientists then look at the physical (including geological) evidence around them—scrambling, if necessary, to support their philosophical framework.

As Christians, however, be believe that human beings are a special creation by God, a fully developed and unique "kind" as described in Genesis 1. As Christians we believe that the universe we see around us is a product of an almighty Creator who fashioned this universe to reflect His intelligence, beauty, love, compassion, and design. (We believe that the creation has been marred by the fall, but that it still reflects its Creator.) Christians believe that men and women are made "in the image of God" and reflect God in special ways. Only we are capable of having fellowship with God and worshipping Him. Only we are capable of those thoughts and actions that make us unique among all life in the universe. Christians also believe that the physical evidence around us in the universe is consistent with the biblical revelation of God, the Creator, Sustainer, and Savior. With R. Laird Harris we can conclude with confidence:

"It is our belief that Genesis is true. It is part of that wonderfully beneficent book, the Bible. Furthermore these very records are referred to by Christ who obviously put His seal of approval on them (Matt. 19:4,5). Genesis speaks only in general terms, it is true. But it says something. And that something is in line with the rest of the Bible's message —that we are both children of God in our spirits and formed of clay in our bodies. We are like the organisms of nature and integrated closely with the processes of nature. But we are not blood brothers to the brute. 'Dust thou art, and unto dust shalt thou return' was not spoken of the soul. In that our creation was given a special dignity, we are honored to be creatures in the image of God. Heaven is our proper home as fellowship is our highest goal. Any view that dims that fellowship and damns that hope is reminiscent of the temptation through which Adam and Eve fell in the Garden."[22]

CHAPTER EIGHT

Natural Disasters and the Design of God

Left: Giant surf is reminiscent of the raging waters of the great flood.
Right: Sedimentary rock formation, perhaps a remnant of the flood of Noah.

As we have mentioned before in passing, the earth's crust consists of a number of different layers or strata which vary widely as to type, thickness, composition, distribution, combination, and fossil content. Rock, the general name for the material of which strata are made, can be of different composition. *Igneous* rocks are solidified magma, or lava, molten rock from beneath the earth which rose to or near the surface, cooled, and hardened. *Sedimentary* rocks are produced from the compression of sediments such as clay, sand, and gravel. *Metamorphic* rocks result from changes in preexisting rocks which are subjected to (usually sudden) tremendous heat and/or pressure. There are other types of rocks (such as sandstones, shales, conglomerates, limestone, and evaporites) but most can be classified in some way under the three main categories above. Given that the strata exist and that we can determine the causes of the different kinds of rock, the questions before creationists and evolutionists are: when, how, and why did the strata come to be as we see them today?

Biblical data give us keys for understanding the formation of the strata. "Biblical *catastrophism,*" as we shall see, provides the most logical and coherent explanation of the rock phenomena in our world today. We will demonstrate this by constructing a catastrophic model (using the biblical outline), compare it to the evolution, or *uniformitarian* model,

How was the immense Grand Canyon formed? How did the Colorado River cut through the thousands of feet of rock to form the largest gorge in North America? Evolutionists must postulate millions of years of sedimentation and then millions of years of gorge-cutting by water. Catastrophism does not require such a time span.

and then compare both with the geological record we actually observe on the earth.

When Did the Strata Come to Be?

Our first question deals with the age of the strata. Here we will define the two terms we used above, catastrophism and uniformitarianism. In geology, *catastrophism* is the general view that the geological formations we see today are primarily the result of one or more large catastrophes. Catastrophism holds that the fossil records and the many strata could have been formed in a relatively short period of time. Geologists who are catastrophists assume that the local or regional disasters we see in the world today are very small in comparison to the enormous destructive forces that formed the geological record before recorded history; these local events, however, can give us explanations for how the solid geological data we have today came about. Catastrophists do not necessarily view the strata as a time line that chronicles the history of the earth and the evolution of life in order.

Geological *uniformitarianism* is the general view that the geological formations we see today are the result of the same natural and environmental phenomena we have around us every day. Change happens only over a very long period of time. Fossils and different kinds of rock are formed over thousands, perhaps even millions, of years. Uniformitarianism holds that the fossil records and the many layers were formed over an extremely long period of time. Geologists who are uniformitarians say that "the present is the key to the past." Uniformitarians believe that the strata represent a time line that chronicles, in order, the history of the earth and the evolution of life. Henry Morris notes some ambiguities in the two terms:

"Now the evolution model is usually associated with uniformitarianism and the creation model with catastrophism. This association does not preclude the possibility that *local* catastrophes can occur within the broad framework of evolutionary uniformitarianism. Nor does it suggest that catastrophism rejects the normal uniform operation of natural laws and processes during most of earth history. Creationists believe in general uniformitarianism as an evidence of the Creator's providential maintenance of the laws. He created in the beginning. On the other hand, certain catastrophists actually deny the existence of a Creator, attributing past cataclysms to purely natural causes. Thus the two terms are flexible and to some extent indicate differences in degree rather than kind."[1]

Sir Charles Lyell (1797-1875), Scottish geologist and the "father" of uniformitarianism.

There is a mutual attraction between geological uniformitarians and biological evolutionists. Both postulate enormous amounts of time as the only mechanism by which the geological strata could have accumulated and evolution could have taken place. It should be no wonder, then, that most evolutionists are uniformitarians, and most uniformitarians are evolutionists. *Encyclopaedia Britannica* recognizes this interdependency, noting it in regard to Darwin and Lyell:

"Darwin denied great and sudden changes in the modification of organic species, preferring to believe that major changes in the organic world are the summation of a host of minute mutations. This gradualism, in turn, required a very long, if indefinite, span of geological time."[2]

However, if, as we propose to show in this chapter, catastrophism answers the *when, how*, and *why* questions of geology better than uniformitarianism does, then there is no need to postulate an extremely old earth and extremely ancient life on earth. (We have already dismissed the evolution model in the previous four chapters, so uniformitarianism remains our lone obstacle to a relatively young earth and biblical creationist model.)

We conclude, then, that while the exact date at which the strata were formed is untestable, the only necessity for postulating an ancient earth and a long period of strata formation is (1) to substantiate a uniformitarian presupposition, and (2) to support the general theory of evolution.* As Bible-believing Christians, we accept neither reason. The Bible clearly states (as we shall discuss below and in chapter nine) that the entire earth was cataclysmically altered by a great flood in the time of Noah. The Bible also clearly states that life was created by God in its various "kinds," and that humans were God's special creation, in His own image. To answer our *when* question: We are not sure *when*, but there is little evidence either biblically or scientifically to postulate the

---

*Progressive creationism can fit the framework of an ancient earth or a considerably younger one.

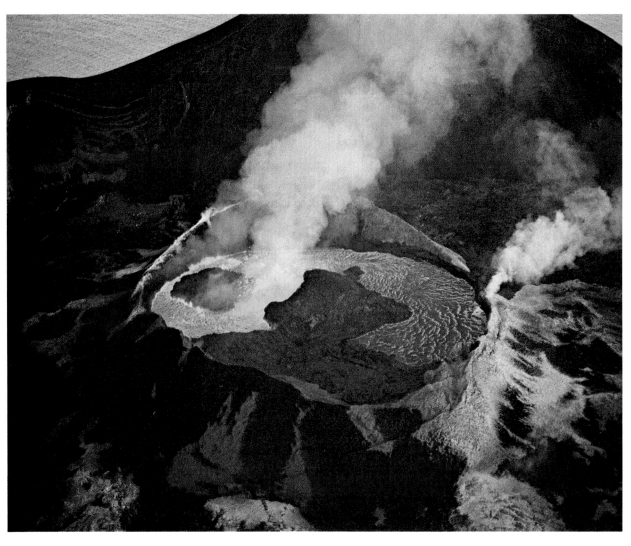

ancient origin or long time span of development for the geological strata we see today.

How Did the Strata Come to Be?

As Christians acquainted with the biblical record and with the general geological evidence, we believe that the strata developed over a relatively short period of time, being precipitated by the universal flood which destroyed the world as it was known at that time. We accept the biblical account of Noah, the ark, and the flood of judgment on the wickedness of mankind. We also accept the geological evidence of a cataclysmic flood which caused massive changes in the earth's crust and in life on earth. (In chapter nine we will discuss evidence of a universal flood other than just geological data.) The Genesis account of the flood in Noah's time gives us one picture of the universality of the flood:

"In the six hundredth year of Noah's life, in the second month, on the seventeenth day of the month, on the same day all the fountains of the great deep burst open, and the floodgates of the sky were opened. And the rain fell upon the earth for forty days and forty nights. On the very same day Noah and Shem and Ham and Japheth, the sons of Noah, and Noah's wife and the three wives of his sons with them, entered the ark, they and every beast after its kind, and all the cattle after their kind, and every creeping thing that creeps on the earth after its kind, and every bird after its kind, all sorts of birds. So they went into the ark to Noah, two by two of all flesh in which was the breath of life. And those that entered, male and female of all flesh, entered as God had commanded him; and the Lord closed it behind him. Then the flood came upon the earth for forty days; and the water increased and lifted up the ark, so that it rose above the earth. And the water prevailed and increased greatly upon the earth; and the ark floated on the surface of the water. And the water prevailed more and more upon the earth, so that all the high mountains everywhere under the heavens were covered. The water prevailed fifteen cubits higher, and the mountains were covered. And all flesh that moved on the earth perished, birds and cattle and beasts and

Left: A local catastrophe, the volcanic eruption on Surtsey of September 3, 1964.
Right: The power of water to carry materials along with it and to carve through rock is immense.

every swarming thing that swarms upon the earth, and all mankind; of all that was on the dry land, all in whose nostrils was the breath of the spirit of life, died. Thus He blotted out every living thing that was upon the face of the land, from man to animals to creeping things and to birds of the sky, and they were blotted out from the earth; and only Noah was left, together with those that were with him in the ark. And the water prevailed upon the earth one hundred and fifty days."[3]

From the above and other biblical passages relating to the flood we can gather the following evidence for a universal, globe-wide deluge which destroyed all life except for that saved aboard the ark. First, God said that He would destroy all people everywhere for their wickedness. The flood could not have been local or even regional and still destroy every human being (Genesis 6:7). Second, the water was said to reach fifteen cubits (22½ feet to 30 feet) higher than the highest mountains. Even if the local mountains around Mesopotamia were meant, the water would still have been deep enough to inundate the entire globe. Third, according to the Bible, the flood was God's judgment against human wickedness (2 Peter 3, etc.). God's judgment was on the whole human race, and so the whole human race was destroyed in that judgment. A local flood would do serious injustice to the righteousness of God and the clear meaning of the passage. The *Wycliffe Bible Encyclopaedia* notes seven different reasons that the flood must have been universal, and then also points out that a "local flood" idea was never popular among biblical scholars until the ascendency of modern geology:

"It is a significant commentary on the clarity of the biblical testimony to the universality of the Flood that no known commentator, Jewish or Christian, ever suggested the local-flood view before A.D. 1655, and that even then the view found scarcely any supporters until after the rise of modern geology in the middle of the 19th century."[4]

There are also geological reasons for believing in a universal flood. The very strata and rock formations uniformitarians use to support their view more consistently and accurately support the biblical universal

flood view. Below we will survey quickly the evidence from fossils, strata, and types of rock.

Michelangelo's picture of the judgment of God on all mankind through the flood (Genesis 7:20-24).

Fossils

Three factors concerning the fossil record point to the universality of the flood: the number of fossils, the formation of fossils, and the location of fossils.

Both scattered fossils and gigantic fossil beds are located around the world, in all climates and all altitudes. There are fossils in Death Valley in California, the lowest elevation on the North American continent. There are fossils on the tops of high mountain ranges around the world. There are fossils in the tropical jungles. There are fossils in the polar regions. The presence of fossils, and often of large deposits, in almost every area of the world is a testimony to the universality of the flood. (See chapter six for more on fossils.)

Uniformitarians postulate that fossils are formed over an extremely long period of time, under stable conditions. Dead plants or animals are slowly covered with sediment, slowly have pressure exerted on them, and slowly petrify. This produces fossils, or so say the uniformitarians. However, with those same conditions in existence today, we should be able to see fossils forming today. Such is not the case. The uniformitarians can point to nothing in the present world as the "key" to the past where fossils are concerned. In fact, the evidence actually points to catastrophe as the origin of fossils.

Morris summarizes how fossilization points to catastrophism:

"There are a number of different ways by which fossils can be produced and preserved. In every case, they must be formed rapidly, or else the forces of erosion, bacterial decay, weathering, or other disintegrative processes will destroy them before the fossilization process is complete. Fossil-forming processes include: (1) preservation of bones or soft parts by induration (compact burial); (2) formation of casts or molds; (3) petrification; (4) cementation of tracks or other impressions; (5) freezing; (6) carbonization (e.g., coal).

"Although some have visualized fossilization as a slow process, brought about by gradual application of heat, pressure, chemical replacement,

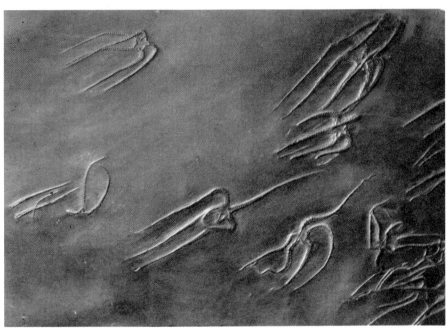

Right: Brittle sea star fossils, still showing the effects of a strong current of water out of which they were trapped.
Below: A lobster, with its tracks, fossilized in sedimentary rock.

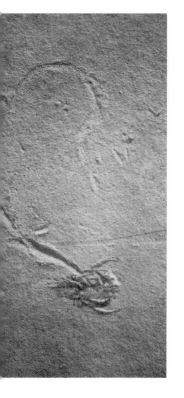

etc., it should be obvious that the actual formation of potential fossils in the first place, before other processes can start to work on them at all, requires rapid and compact burial of the organisms concerned, and this requires catastrophism."[5]

So, we find that catastrophism fits the fossil record better than uniformitarianism.

Strata

Our second consideration is the formation of the strata, or layers of rock built up on the crust of the earth. As we discussed at the beginning of the chapter, there are several different types of rock, formed in different ways. We will discuss types of rock below. How those types of rocks become layered refers to the types of strata we find. Since our discussion of strata as testimony to catastrophism rather than to uniformitarianism is necessarily short, we will refer only to two issues. (Further information on strata is available by reading other books in the recommended reading list.) We will discuss (1) the evidence that the strata were laid continuously, without interruption, and (2) the evidence that fossil forms, assigned by geologists and evolutionists to different geological "ages," are found in the same stratum, indicating that the life forms lived at the same time.

131

Each stratum varies in width from less than an inch to several inches. The only way geologists can differentiate between two adjoining strata (ignoring the fossil evidence) is by the "stratification planes" which are present at the intersection of the layers. Morris notes how the stratification planes are formed:

"The adjacent strata may be of the same material, contain the same types of fossils and look very much like it. The planes between them, however, indicate that some slight difference must have intervened to denote a break — either a brief time-lapse in deposition, or a slight change in one or more of the characteristics of the sediment-forming flow."[6]

Fossilized ammonites against a piece of wood where they were pushed by strong sea currents.

There are specific characteristics of stratification planes that separate strata from widely different time periods. Picture it this way: Sedimentary action, for example, deposits a layer of strata three inches thick. The cause of the sedimentation is taken away (the river changes course, the lake dries up, etc.). For a long period of time no sedimentation takes place at that location. A stratification plane is formed as the top surface of the stratum. If the stratum contains fossils, they will be fossils of animals and/or plants that were contemporaries during the time the stratum was deposited. After this long time period, sedimentation resumes (the river changes back, rainfall and snow runoff refill the lake, etc.). The stratification plane separates the original stratum from this new stratum. The new stratum, if it contains fossils, will likewise contain fossils of contemporaneous animals and/or plants.

Given the above model, a geologist studying the strata thousands of years later should be able to "decode" the message of the strata. He should assume that the higher stratum was formed after the lower one. If the fossils in the two strata are markedly different, he might suspect that the strata were laid at different time periods. He could assume a long separation between strata only if the strafication planes between the strata show evidence of erosion or wear (the geological terms for that are disconformity, paraconformity, or unconformity). The only way the stratification planes can be protected from erosion is by being covered with the next stratum.

Is that what geologists find? No. On the contrary, most of the stratification planes between stratum layers are remarkably free from any deterioration at all. Although stratification is fairly complicated, Morris sums up the evidence this way:

"If there is no observable time break between these [geological ages], either in terms of physical unconformities or changes in faunas, then there is no such break anywhere! In other words, the stratigraphic record shows that each 'age' merges gradually and imperceptibly into

Right: A mass "grave" of many kinds of fossilized bones. Perhaps these graves were caused by strong water currents, such as those occurring during the Flood. Below: Fossilized deep sea coral, found not in marine strata but in a coral bed.

the next 'age.' One cannot really determine strictly where one age starts and another ends. In other words *there are no time breaks; the time is continuous.*

"Now recall again that each of the individual rock units shows evidence of rapid formation. The fossil deposits, which date the rock units, all show evidence of rapid formation. If there are no time breaks between the various ages (or, more precisely, between the various stratigraphic systems which supposedly denote the various ages), then it seems rigidly necessary to conclude that the entire assemblage of rock units constituting the geologic column shows evidence of rapid formation."[7]

There is abundant evidence, admitted by evolutionists and creationists alike, that fossilized life forms which are supposed to belong to different geologic ages are sometimes found together or in reverse order in the strata. Evolutionists and creationists differ in explaining those anomalies, however.

Evolutionists usually insist that under- or overthrusting of strata is responsible for finding fossil life forms in reverse order from the evolution model. They explain fossil life forms from different "ages" in the same strata by saying that mini-catastrophes occurred which jumbled the strata and formed new anomalous strata. They still insist

PINK HYDROZOAN CORAL
Genus: Stylaster

that their basic evolution and geologic model holds firm—simple plant forms first, complex plant forms second, marine invertebrates third, marine vertebrates fourth, amphibians fifth, reptiles sixth, and mammals (including humans) last.

Creationists, on the other hand, reject the evolutionists' explanations. Creationists agree that the geologic column represents the normal manner or order in which fossil materials were deposited. This fits with the catastrophic model. The waters of the flood, rising swiftly, overtook different life forms at different times during a very short period. The marine plant life and marine microorganisms, simple to complex, were deposited first. As the waters became polluted from the flooding and

This Hawaiian "lavascape" is of recently formed igneous rock.

from cataclysmic events on the earth such as volcanos, the marine animal life succumbed and was deposited. Amphibians, being closest to the water, died and were deposited next. Reptiles, with little ability to escape and with mostly low-level habitats were next. Warm-blooded animals, especially small ones that could not travel far or quickly, followed. Finally, large warm-blooded animals and those humans who were unable to escape the initial reaches of the flood were deposited. Most others who died from the flood probably were destroyed through decomposition and the destructive force of the waters before they could be deposited into sediment layers and fossilized.

Creationists do not have to drum up fanciful explanations for anomalies in the fossil and stratification layers. Since the majority of sedimentation and stratification took place over a very short period of time, as a result of the great flood, it would not be at all impossible for life forms to be mixed up or for the order of sedimentation to be reversed in certain areas. The true stratification and fossil record is completely consistent with the catastrophic model. Space limitations preclude our discussing this further here, but there are sound creationist answers to the evolutionary explanations of the strata and stratification anomalies. (We refer the reader to the excellent discussion in Morris's *Scientific Creationism*, cited above.)

Biological Cross Section of the Grand Canyon

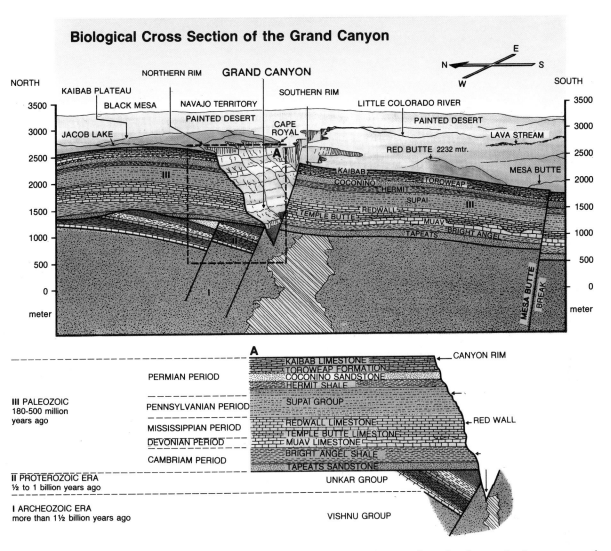

Above: A cross-section of the Grand Canyon presents several problems for the evolutionist:
a. regular strata over broad areas of hundreds of square kilometers;
b. absence of certain strata (which would represent hundreds of millions of years of evolution) without any trace of erosion;
c. occasional alternating of several Cambrian and Mississippian strata (each of which is supposed to represent a particular period of time);
d. presence of highly developed organisms in very "old" strata (Proterozoic). The catastrophe model has no problems with these.

Finally, let us turn to the types of rocks formed. As we mentioned before, rocks can be described in three major categories: igneous, metamorphic, and sedimentary. In our brief survey, we shall see that each kind of rock is formed very quickly, and presents no problem to our catastrophic model.

Igneous rock is formed when magmas (rock materials heated to liquid forms) are pushed to or close to the surface of the earth's crust. There they quickly cool and become solid rock. Lava-flows from modern volcanos are evidence of this.

Geologists are unable to find metamorphic rocks being formed anywhere on the earth today. That fact makes it difficult to determine how they were formed in the past. A metamorphic rock is one that used to be a sedimentary rock (such as limestone), but which changed into a different form (as into marble). Geologists surmise that both tremendous heat and pressure are necessary for the formation of metamorphic rock. This is consistent with catastrophism.

Sedimentary rocks are most important to geological investigation both because they are the most numerous rock forms and because they are the rocks within which we find fossils. Uniformitarians assume that the normal, slow processes of sedimentation which we observe around us today are the same processes that in times past produced sedimentary rock. Sedimentation today, however, does not solidify into rock. There are several different types of sedimentary rock. We will discuss just one below as representative of the problems uniformitarians and evolutionists have with explaining sedimentation into rock in their own geologic models.

Coal, evolutionists and creationists agree, is the remains of plant life, placed under extreme heat and pressure, and carbonized into rock. As we discussed in chapter five, evolutionists postulate that coal seams are the carbonized remains of successive layers of peat bogs. The peat bogs built upon one another, pressing the older layers beneath them until these hundreds of layers began transforming into coal. Uniformitarians must postulate literally thousands and thousands of years of peat bog formations to account for the large coal beds around the world. Catastrophists have a more reasonable suggestion: the lush tropical antediluvian plant world was cataclysmically destroyed and impacted under great pressure and heat and, in a very short period, produced coal. (Coal can be produced in the laboratory in one hour.) A cataclysm is necessary to kill such a quantity of plant life at once, to account for the drastic change in weather and vegetation after the cataclysm, and to provide the pressure and heat necessary to transform the vegetation into coal.

From the above we have seen that catastrophism is a better explanation for the fossil records, the strata, and the types of rock. Catastrophism took place, according to the Bible, during the great flood of Noah. (See the next chapter for a thorough discussion of that flood.)

The scenario presented by the Bible fits with catastrophism. Genesis 7:11 tells us that at the beginning of the flood, "all the fountains of the great deep burst open." Across the entire ocean floor, which is the thinnest part of the earth's crust, the catastrophe began on the same day. The entire ocean floor was lifted up. Enormous volcanic explosions took place. Great quantities of liquids (magma, water, etc.) that had been confined under the crust under great pressure broke through. Resultant earthquakes, other geological catastrophes, and tidal waves occurred all over the world.

The "floodgates of the sky" were opened and rain fell for forty days and forty nights, around the world. (The source of all of this water, much more than is present in our atmosphere today, is debated. Several explanations are in harmony both with the Bible and science. Check books in the recommended reading list for further information.)

Simple calculations reveal that the forty-day downpour did not account for all the flood water, which covered the highest mountains (even though the mountains may not have been as high then). Most of the water probably came from subterranean water masses that burst forth from the "fountains of the great deep." The torrential downpour would have caused enormous erosion of the soil and rocks still above water. Soon the water began to run down the slopes to lower levels, carrying the first sedimentary materials, which created a "snowballing" effect and increased the erosion.

Local floods today can give us a tiny picture of what it must have been like. Local rains and floods can wipe out entire villages, cities, and countrysides in a remarkably short time. Boulders weighing several

This petrified tree trunk spans many time-layers of sedimentary rock. According to evolutionists, this is an anomaly, since the sedimentary layers supposedly were deposited separately over a long period of time. The tree trunk would have rotted before the layers could have built up. Catastrophism, on the other hand, postulates the rapid accumulation of sedimentary layers as a result of the flood.

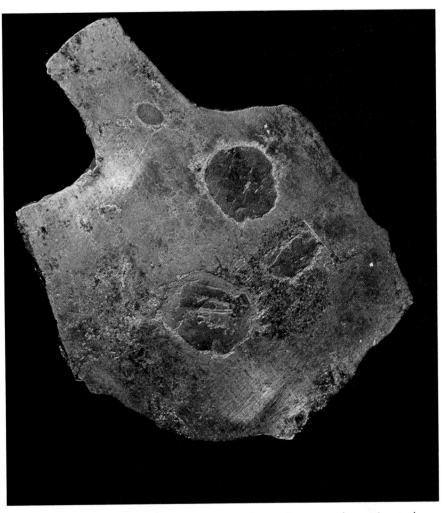

A fossilized meteorite, found in sedimentary rock.

hundred tons can be transported over long distances in a short time. Thousands of tons of material per square kilometer can be picked up by flood waters and deposited elsewhere. Rivers can quickly swell to a depth of several stories, destroying everything in their paths. If a localized catastrophe can do that, what would be the effects of a flood so enormous that it covered the highest mountains and ravaged the earth for almost a year and a half? And what would have been the geological aftermath of such a disaster?

Let's look at a plausible flood model. Such a gigantic cataclysm must have caused tremendous sedimentary activity. Because of the continuous rains, the bursting forth of the "fountains of the deep," the enormous magma eruptions, the tremendous earthquakes, the giant tidal waves, and the shifting of the land, the earth's crust would be brutally battered. The magma and sand churned up by the turbulent water and steam would bury millions of marine invertebrates alive on the bottom of the oceans. The first deposits, then, would contain the remains of marine invertebrates that lived on the ocean floor.

Immediately above these first strata we would expect to find the remains of fish, since they could escape a little longer. We would also find more marine invertebrates.

In the meantime, disaster also struck the land. Ultimately, all land animals would also perish. Although people would try to escape by

137

running, climbing, and swimming, they too would drown in the end, in a few cases being buried relatively intact by the turbulent masses of earth and water. The earth's surface would be eroded by the floods. Uprooted trees and plant life in tangled masses would be shoved by the waters to the sea.

The land masses themselves would undergo tremendous changes. Rocks would bounce and crack in the turbulence, disintegrating into gravel and sand. Enormous seas of mud and rocks would race downstream and overtake plant and animal remains, dragging them along.

As the waters calmed, these sediments would slowly settle again. Dissolved chemicals would settle in thick layers at various times and places.

Right: This sea urchin was buried alive and became part of the sedimentary rock. Below: Cross-section from an anomalous plant fossil in coal formations.

Thick sedimentary layers would be formed all over the world. Under the great forces of cataclysm, they would form into fossil-bearing sedimentary rock and deposits of coal.

According to hydrodynamic selectivity, water so saturated with sediments would deposit those sediments in horizontally stacked layers (strata). The sequence of those layers would be determined by the specific gravity and degree of rounding of the formative particles. In just a few months' time, a large number of sedimentary layers could be formed in various parts of the world, sometimes to a depth of more than a kilometer.

The Geologic Column

The result of the great flood would be a "geologic column" formed, not slowly and gradually over a period of millions of years, but rather very rapidly during and immediately after the flood. In subsequent ages, its shape was finalized. It is important to remember that the settling of the strata could continue for a period of time after the actual flood; petrification of the strata and the organisms they contain required a much longer process than the formation of the strata themselves.

Further, not all strata were formed as a direct result of the flood. It is logical to assume that the virtually fossil-free strata of the Precambrian period were formed before the flood, while at least the strata of the Tertiary and Quaternary, as well as part (and according to some, all) of the strata of the Mesozoic periods must date from after the flood.

The geologic time scales postulated by evolutionists is useful only as a general indication of the *sequence* in which the strata are formed. It is not useful as a "calendar" of events and evolution. It is striking that this sequence agrees with what we would expect on the basis of our flood model, while at the same time, the flood model resolves the problems inherent in the evolutionary time scale. Only catastrophism, including the flood model, offers a reasonable explanation for the existence of

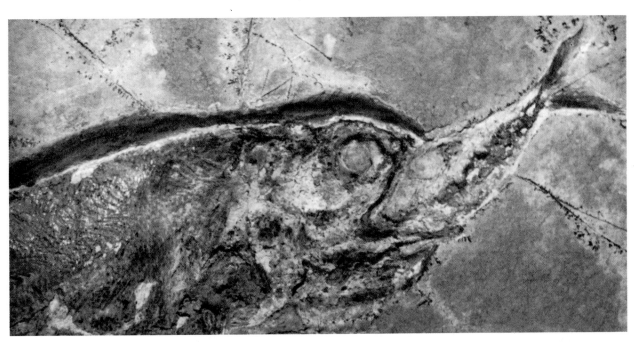

This fossilized fish did not have time to swallow its prey before it was overcome and buried by sediment.

many large "graves," where the remains of hundreds of thousands of animals are found in one location.

The uniformitarian model can explain one way in which the first strata would contain only marine organisms, while land animals are found only in the higher strata. The flood model can also explain the sequence. However, only the flood model can provide a satisfactory explanation for the occasional occurrence of land organisms in the lower strata.

The evolutionary model is unable to account for the lack of evolutionary transitional forms in the fossil record. The flood model, on the other hand, expects to find representatives of all groups of marine animals, which we will find in the sea today, as well as of some extinct groups, in the earliest strata. Immediately above the virtually fossil-free strata of the Precambrian, we find those of the Cambrian and Ordovician, in which almost all groups of marine animals, and even virtually all classes of the animal kingdom, are represented in fossil form. The inability to explain this on the basis of the evolutionary theory is one of the major shortcomings of the uniformitarian model. Morris notes:

"In other words, the fossil world was much like our own world. If the present is really the key to the past, as uniformitarians allege, why should this be surprising? In the present world are found one-celled

A fold in the Old Red Sandstone strata on the English coast, evidence of extreme pressure and force which worked to disrupt uniform sedimentary stratification.

organisms, marine invertebrates, fish, amphibians, reptiles, birds, mammals, and men. The only reason to think that all should not have been living contemporaneously in the past is the assumption of evolution. Apart from this premise, there is no reason to doubt that man lived at the same time as the dinosaurs and trilobites."[8]

Our combined observations suggest that the larger part of the "geologic column" was formed during one worldwide catastrophe. We have to think back only to the fossil tree trunks that sometimes lie through several strata for ten or twenty meters, indicating that these strata must have been formed at approximately the same time. Further, some rivers, such as the Colorado River as it cuts through the Grand Canyon, could have cut their channels (some to a depth of one and one-half kilometers) only while the lower strata were still soft. This must have occurred rapidly.

Sometimes disconformities are found (the sequence of the strata is normal, but one or more strata are missing). It is assumed that those missing strata once existed. In the flood model, that erosion was caused by water. Such an assumption means that there was a time lapse between the formation of the lower strata and those above the missing stratum or strata. In the flood model, that time lapse would not have to be more than a few days or weeks.

140

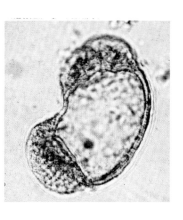

But what is striking is that it is possible to reconstruct the entire geological column from the lowest strata to the surface in spite of these disconformities. In other words, the disconformities are local anomalies. Their limited occurrence means that, apart from local disturbances that caused such disconformities, many strata were nevertheless formed rapidly and simultaneously around the world. Such evidence all points to the flood model.

Conclusion

From our overview, we have seen that uniformitarianism and evolution go hand in hand. Both uniformitarians and evolutionists postulate that

Above: Fossilized pollen found in Proterozoic age strata in the Grand Canyon. It does not fit the evolutionary scale to find such fossils in Precambrian rock. Right: The Lewis Overthrust, which has no characteristics (abrasion, etc.) associated with a true overthrust. When evolutionists find strata which appear to have been deposited out of the proper evolutionary sequence, they postulate overthrusting as its cause. Below: The controversial finds along the Paluxy (Texas) River, of dinosaur and human footprints, apparently contemporaneous.

chance plus matter plus time can produce anything and everything. If, however, there is a God who created the universe and everything in it (see chapters one, two, and three), and if the evolution model does not fit the evidence (see chapters four through seven), then uniformitarian presuppositions are unnecessary. In fact, we find that uniformitarian geology does not fit the geological evidence. Catastrophism, which is consistent with theism and the biblical record, does fit the evidence.

We will see in chapter nine how the flood inundated the entire earth. The flood was God's judgment on the wickedness of humankind. In chapter ten we will see how the world in which we live today reflects the aftermath of that great flood. Finally, we will see how the events of the flood so long ago have practical and eternal significance for humanity today.

ሉበቶመየ፡ቶለጥሪሉ፡ሀዋነ　　　　ግኔሠጋሰ፡ተሰዉ፡ሰለዖለዘሪ

ሐቶቅበ፡ደ፡ኢሣቶ፡ፆ፡ሊ፡ለ፡ዘ　　　　፡ሕበወ፡ዕ፡ነቂ፡ቀቃጷ፡ታጎለ፡ቶ

ግል፡ኢ፡ቶ፡ለ፡ጠ፡ጌ፡ሦየ፡ለ፡መሰ፡ 　　　ለዘዖ፡ቶ፡ጊ፡ለበ፡ ቀ፡ለሐ፡ግ፡መለ

　　　ᛧ ⵀ፡ዱጷ፡ ፡ለለᛁ　　　　ᛁ ሣቂ፡ለበየለዘ፡ነሐመ፡ጋሐዉ

CHAPTER NINE

Noah and the Great Flood

Left: An Ethiopian manuscript illumination of Noah and the ark. Right: A portion of the Gilgamesh Epic, the Babylonian flood account.

The biblical story of Noah and the great flood is a testimony to the righteous judgment and the grace of God, the Creator of the universe. It is not a primitive myth, nor is it a fanciful legend told to entertain. It tells of rampant evil and wickedness in the world, and of God's absolute judgment against that evil and wickedness. It tells of His infinite undeserved kindness, or grace, toward eight people whose faith in God saved them from the judgment of death meted out to every other inhabitant of the earth. The aftermath of the flood tells us of the protection and immense power of God, who has promised that He will never again destroy the world by water. The rainbow is an "icon," or pictorial reminder of God's promise to Noah and his family.

The great flood of Noah is an historical record of God's judgment and salvation in action with mankind. In this chapter we will discuss flood traditions from around the world and their parallels to the biblical account, the ark of Noah, the gathering and care of the animals, and the other biblical passages that show the purpose and typology of the great flood of Noah.

Flood Traditions

The Gilgamesh Epic, including its lengthy flood story, is the story best known outside the Bible concerning the early history of the created world. Lutheran theologian Alfred Rehwinkel traces the history of the finding of the Gilgamesh Epic:

"The most remarkable of all Flood stories outside the Bible is the Babylonian account of the Flood, which was brought with thousands of other clay tablets from the ancient library of Assurbanipal in Nineveh to the British Museum, where it was accidentally discovered by George Smith, a British orientalist, in 1872. As early as 1845 Layard had begun to dig in a mound which proved to be the site of Nineveh, the ancient capital of Assyria. In this mound he found the ruins of two palaces that had been destroyed by fire. One turned out to be that of Sennacherib, known to us from the Second Book of Kings. The other was the ruined

Right: Most North American Indians have flood legends, including (far right) the Alaskan Eskimos.
Below: Gilgamesh, tamer of wild animals.

palace of Assurbanipal, who reigned from 668 to 626 B.C. From these palatial ruins, especially those of Assurbanipal's palace, he brought back a number of treasures, including about 20,000 clay tablets and fragments of clay tablets covered with cuneiform inscriptions. The work of sorting and deciphering these tablets was a difficult one. Mr. Smith was engaged to make copies of the inscriptions of the more important tablets for foreign scholars, and in doing so he acquired a thorough knowledge of the cuneiform script, which was at that time still little understood. While engaged at this task, he accidentally came across a small fragment of a tablet on which he read these words: 'The mountain of Nisir stopped the ship. I sent forth a dove, and it left. The dove went and turned, and a resting place it did not find, and it returned.'

"Smith perceived at once that these lines resembled an incident in the account of the Flood of Noah as recorded in Genesis, and he began an untiring search for the missing fragment. His labors were rewarded beyond expectation. He found not only many fragments of this account of the Flood but parts of two other copies. When he had assembled all the fragments that he could find, he made a careful translation of the whole text, in which there were, of course, still many gaps. He published the results of this most remarkable discovery before a meeting of the Society of Biblical Archaeology on December 30, 1872."[1]

The Gilgamesh flood story tells how the gods decided to bring a flood on mankind, and how Ea, the god of wisdom, told Utnapishtim (corresponding to the Noah figure of the biblical story) of this decision by saying: "Tear down (thy) house, build a ship! Abandon thy possessions, seek to save life!...Cause to go up into the ship the seed of all living creatures. The ship which thou shalt build, its measurements shall be accurately measured." The account then tells of how Utnapishtim built his boat, loaded the animals on, and shut the ark up against the torrential rains. After the rains subsided, Utnapishtim, like the biblical Noah, sent birds out as scouts, to see if it was safe to disembark. The last bird he sent was a raven: "The raven went away, and when she saw that the

Right: Jack Dabner's model of the ark of Noah, with the roof removed for interior viewing. Below: A clay relief made from an Egyptian cylinder seal which depicts a boat.

waters had abated, she ate, she flew about, she cawed, and did not return. Then I sent forth everything to the four winds and offered a sacrifice."

The Gilgamesh account of the flood bears striking similarities to the biblical account. Nineteenth-century higher critics were quick to seize on the earlier written Babylonian account as the true source of the biblical account. The differences between the two accounts, however, are also striking. There are numerous logistically impossible or impractical assertions concerning the construction, dimensions, and use of the Babylonian "ark." There are no such problems with the biblical ark, as we shall see in a later section of this chapter. There are other serious problems with the Gilgamesh flood story too numerous and detailed to cover here. We assume that the Gilgamesh account is the imperfectly transmitted tradition of a true but distant occurrence which Moses, in writing Genesis, preserved perfectly because of the intermediary agency of God the Holy Spirit. Perhaps Moses and the writer of the Gilgamesh account had some common sources of information or tradition. That does not take away from the amazing accuracy and inspiration of the biblical account. Bernard Ramm summarizes:

"Heidel's work [*The Gilgamesh Epic and Old Testament Parallels*, 1946],...must be consulted in any serious study of the flood. Heidel shows the great contrasts between the Babylonian and the Hebrew accounts. The Hebrew account is sane, moral, theistic, whereas the Babylonian account is frequently silly or grotesque, and polytheistic. Heidel also tackles the lions of criticism and defends the unity of the flood account."[2]

Traditions of a mighty and universal flood are found all over the world, which is strong circumstantial evidence that all humanity once fell victim to a "judgment by water," and that the only survivors, Noah and his family, then repopulated the world. Here is a list of just a few representatives of the worldwide flood tradition.

Asia and India

Flood stories are found in the folklore of even remote tribes on the Indian peninsula, including those of the Kamars, those in Kashmir, and in Assam. The Karens of Thailand report that a brother and sister were saved on a boat, and then repopulated the world. The Vietnamese tradition talks of a brother and sister, also, who were saved in a great "chest" which also contained two of every kind of animal. In a Chinese tradition, Fah-he escaped from the flood with his wife, three sons, and three daughters, from whom the entire population of the modern world

was descended. Japanese tradition recounts that their islands rose like jewels from the Pacific, which achieved its present form after a great deluge. These are just a few of the flood traditions abounding throughout the tribal cultures of Asia and India.

Australia and the Pacific

The Australian aborigines have flood stories which say that God sent the flood as judgment on the wickedness of mankind. The Hawaiians say that a long time after the first man, Kumukonna, all of mankind became completely wicked. The only righteous man was Nu-u, who was saved from the flood which inundated the land. God left the rainbow as a token of his forgiveness of Nu-u and his family. Natives of Fiji tell that only eight persons were saved from a devastating flood. The Battaks of Sumatra recite that their creator, Debata, was angry with mankind for its evil and determined to destroy it by flood. All of mankind died except for one couple, who took refuge on the peak of a high mountain and were forgiven by Debata. There are many other flood stories among the multiple island cultures of Australia and the Pacific.

North and South America

Native inhabitants of both North and South America consistently have flood stories in their traditional myths. Alaskans tell the story that the "father" of their tribe lived "toward the rising sun." Warned by a vision

Above: Drawing of the ark from a taped description by an Armenian who claimed to have seen the ark on the slopes of Mt. Ararat when he was a small boy (1902 and 1904).
Below: Moses was set adrift as a baby by his mother in an "ark" of bullrushes.

A cross-section of the Titanic, which sank on its maiden voyage in 1912. The Titanic and the ark had approximately the same displacement (46,000 and 43,000 tons, respectively).

that a flood would destroy all life on th earth, he built a raft upon which he was able to save his whole family and all the animals. The Athapascan Indians, on the west coast of North America, have a flood tradition. Their tradition teaches that it rained day and night until "the sky fell and the land was not." All life — plant, animal, and human — was destroyed. Then dry land and life were created again by the Earth-god Nagaitche. Arizona Indians tell that a great flood destroyed all people except Montezuma and his friend, a coyote. After the flood subsided, the Great Spirit used Montezuma to help repopulate the earth with animals and people. That story is fairly representative of Indian myths across North America. In South America, the Brazilian natives believed in a worldwide flood of judgment. In Peru a tradition states that before the time of the Incas, all the people were drowned except for six who were saved on a raft. Even at the tip of South America, in Tierra del Fuego, the natives preserved the tradition that mankind was judged for wickedness and that all life was destroyed except for a few people who sought refuge on top of the highest mountain.

Europe

The ancient Druids taught that in judgment a great fire split the earth so that all of the seas swept over the earth and killed all life except for one wise man, his family, and the animals he had gathered and placed in his

147

barge. The ancient Greeks possessed a flood tradition: Homer wrote of the "rainbow that the son of Kronos set in the clouds" after a great flood. The Latin poet Ovid preserved an ancient version of the flood story in his *Metamorphoses*. Remnants of a flood tradition survive in the legends of Finland, Lapland, and almost every culture in Europe.

Africa

Plato recorded a statement of an Egyptian priest that the gods purified the earth by covering it with a flood. In the Sudan, the natives call Lake Chad *Bahr el Nuh*, the Lake of Noah. Natives in western Nigeria believed that the chief of all the gods, Sango, destroyed all of mankind

Right: P. Ucello: Diluvio universale. *The people who refused to believe Noah's warnings while he was building the ark tried desperately to get in once the rain began.*
Below: Frenchman Fernand Navarra climbed Mt. Ararat several times in search of the ark. On July 7, 1955, he found this piece of hand-tooled wood beneath the ice. He is convinced it is a part of the ark.

except for one of his servants because of their ingratitude toward him. Although there are fewer flood traditions in Africa than in any other part of the world, numerous tribal groups throughout the continent do preserve a tradition of a great flood.

The parallels between the many stories scattered around the world are amazing. They generally agree that (1) there is some provision made (an ark, barge, etc.); (2) all living things are destroyed by water; (3) only a few chosen ones are saved through divine intervention; (4) the flood was judgment against the wickedness of mankind; (5) one person is warned beforehand and is thus able to save himself (and often his family and animals); (6) animals are often saved with the few humans, and birds are often used by the humans to report the end of the flood; (7) the vessel comes to rest on a mountaintop or the people are saved on a mountaintop. Frederick Filby concludes: "The cumulative weight of this evidence is that the present human race has spread from one centre and even from one family—a family who themselves experienced the great Deluge of which every story speaks."[3] Rehwinkel concurs, stating:

"Nature myths have their origin in a great historical fact. We cannot escape the conclusion that these Flood traditions are an indisputable proof that the world catastrophe as described in Genesis is one of the greatest facts of all history. It has left an indelible impression on the memory of the entire human race."[4]

Noah's Ark

In this section we will survey the biblical description of the ark, modern comparisons to the ark, the number and kinds of animals Noah carried with him on the ark, and the logistics of housing and feeding such an array of life. The consistency and logical feasibility of the biblical account cannot be ignored, especially when compared to the sometimes absurd descriptions contained, for example, in the Gilgamesh epic.

Utnapishtim, hero of the Gilgamesh epic, didn't have much chance of survival if he depended on the ark described in the Babylonian

An expedition on Mt. Ararat, in search of Noah's ark.

tradition. His ark was described in the epic as a cube, with sides of 60 meters, with six decks dividing it into seven stories. Such a cube shape would tumble slowly and contiuously in the seas of the flood. Noah's ark looked very different. The Hebrew word translated "ark" is *tebah* and means chest, or box, and is used of only one other vessel in the Bible: the bulrush basket in which Moses was saved as a baby.[5]

The biblical ark was an oblong, almost rectangular, boxlike barge. The ancient *cubit* measurement varied from about 18 inches to perhaps as much as 24 inches. The dimensions of the ark were somewhere between a minimum of 138 meters by 22½ meters with a height of 13.8 meters and a maximum of 180 meters by 30 meters with a height of 18 meters.

The ark had three decks, each divided into cubicles and compartments. While the dimensions of the compartments are not given in the biblical record, we know that their function was both to separate the animals and to provide what we would today call "bulkheading" for bracing the exterior structure of the ark. It was probably made from cypress wood, and was coated with pitch inside and out, to waterproof it. It had a door and a window which probably ran around the under edge of the entire roof overhang. We are unable to know exactly the type of window meant, since the particular passage is unclear. Ramm notes:

"The most obscure reference is concerning the expression in verse 16.

Does this refer to a ventilation system or to a lighting system, or just to a roof? The American Standard Version reads *light* and puts *roof* in the margin, whereas the Revised Standard Version reverses them and puts *roof* in the text and *light* in the margin. The interpretation about the cubit is just as uncertain. Does it mean that the light system or ventilation system was one cubit wide around the ark, or does it mean that the ark is so to slope as to come within a cubit of closing off the top? The text is too brief to allow us to come to any certain decision."[6]

Noah designed and built the ark over a 120-year period, probably hiring local help as well as using his family members to help. It was a well-built

vessel, the perfect design for surviving cataclysmic waves with a heavy cargo.

Was the ark too large for Noah and his family to attempt to build? Would it have been possible for such "primitive" people to construct such a grand structure? Filby notes:

"Yet even granting all this some may feel that the Ark was too large for early man to have attempted. A survey of the ancient world shows in fact the very reverse. One is constantly amazed at the enormous tasks which our ancestors attempted. The Great Pyramid was not the work of the later Pharaohs; it was the work of the 4th Dynasty—long before Abraham! This pyramid contained over two million blocks of stone each weighing about 2½ tons. Its vast sides, 756 feet long, are set to the points of the compass to an accuracy of a small fraction of one degree! The so-called Colossi of Memnon again are not of recent times—they belong to the 18th Dynasty of Egypt. Cut from blocks of sandstone they weigh 400 tons each and were brought 600 miles to their present position. Among the remains of that most ancient Empire in Greece— Mycenae—is the 'Treasury of Atreus.' Above its entrance rests a huge stone lintel 28 feet across. It weighs 120 tons! The Temple of Jupiter at Baalbek is later, but it is staggering to find in the retaining wall three great blocks of stone each weighing about 700 tons...."[7]

Although Noah and his family, with hired help, were capable of building such an ark, vessels of such dimensions were not built again until almost modern times. The *Titanic* was longer and wider than the ark, but the ark's flat bottom and angular shape gave it a similar displacement: around 43,000 tons to the *Titanic's* 46,000 tons.

In 1604 a Dutchman, Peter Jansz, built two ships which had the same proportions as the ark, but were smaller. Because these small "arks"

Below: A black bear, preparing for hibernation. If many animals on the ark hibernated during the flood, their food and care needs would have been minimal.

150

could carry one-third more cargo than regular ships without requiring any additional crew, they became so successful that they were copied by other builders. Their speed was better than average, but they had poor steering capabilities, which made them unsuitable for use as military vessels. For decades Jansz's type of ship was popular as a cargo carrier.

The Animals on the Ark

Many argue that even though the ark had an enormous cargo capacity, it still was unequal to the task of carrying two of every single animal on the face of the earth, and enough food to sustain them for over one year.

Above: A mural of plant and animal life before the flood.

Such critics miss some important points.

First, Noah did not have to take two of every single kind of animal. Noah had to take only two of each "kind" into the ark. "Kind" is not necessarily the same as "species." (See the discussion in chapter five; even scientists disagree on their definition of "species"). Noah was charged with preserving the various "kinds" of animals living at the time of the flood. He did not have to preserve marine animals, who already lived in water. He did not have to preserve animals that were already extinct. He did not have to preserve each type of animal within each "kind." For example it would be reasonable to think that he had only one "dog kind" couple on the ark. From them could have descended (after the flood) each of the varieties of "dog kinds" we see on earth today, including chihuahuas, great danes, wolves, foxes, etc. Some conservative scholars estimate that the entire animal kingdom could have been represented by "kinds" and have taken up no more than one-fifth of the storage space on the ark. (That figure even allows for the seven pairs of "clean" animals required for sacrifice.)

Second, Noah did not go out and gather the animals himself. The biblical record indicates that God caused the animals to come to Noah. Given supernatural intervention by God, it does not matter whether their transport was instantaneous or took any or all of the 120 years the ark was being built. Most scientists also believe that at one time there was only one land mass, and no separate continents. If that were the situation before the flood of Noah, travel distances would have been much shorter. And if the earth's climate was very different from that after the flood (see chapter eight), and there were no extremes in temperature and climate, then the differences among types of animals within kinds would have been less significant. Given that the earth's topography was much different before it was ravaged by the flood,

151

physical obstacles to the animals' traveling to Noah would be inconsequential.

Third, the food requirements of the animals could have been substantially less than one would think at first. Many of the younger animals would have required a smaller amount of food than full-sized adults. Some animals naturally hibernate or lower their metabolisms given adverse weather conditions (winter, or a year-long flood, for example). Reptiles are especially prone to slower metabolism in colder weather because they are cold-blooded. Such animals would require less food than normal. And, too, there was still four-fifths of the cargo capacity of the ark which could accommodate the animals' food needs.

In concluding this section on the dimensions of the ark and the logistics of boarding and keeping the many animals, we will return to Rehwinkel for a summary:

"This is the history of the Flood as recorded by Moses in the first book of the Bible. To countless millions of all ages this book has been and still is the inspired Word of God, and therefore correct in every detail, also when dealing with natural phenomena and scientific facts. The Bible is not a textbook on geology or any other science, but whenever it touches fields of knowledge belonging to these categories, it is reliable and not merely representing in poetical or allegorical language the

Left: An artist's symbolic portrayal of God's judgment against evil people through the flood.
Right: God declared He would never again destroy the earth through flood. However, judgment is coming and God will judge by fire in the last day (2 Peter 3:12).
Below: An Orthodox icon of Noah.

erroneous, naive, or limited views current at the time when it was written. But the historicity of the Deluge does not depend upon Genesis alone. It is confirmed by other sacred writers of the Bible in both the Old and New Testaments and by Christ Himself. Thus Job refers to the Flood in Chapter 22:15-16.... Or Isaiah 54:9.... And in Luke 3:36. Noah and his son Shem are mentioned in the genealogy of Christ. In Matt. 24:37-38 our Savior refers to the Flood in the following words: 'But as the days of Noah were, so shall also the coming of the Son of Man be; for as in the days that were before the Flood they were eating and drinking, marrying and given in marriage until the day that Noah entered into the ark.' And in Hebrews 11:7 Noah is numbered among the heroes of faith. And Peter refers to Noah and the Flood (1 Peter 3:20) as follows: 'Which sometime were disobedient, when once the long-suffering of God waited in the days of Noah, while the ark was a preparing, wherein few, that is, eight souls were saved by water.' And 2 Peter 2:5: 'And spared not the old word, but saved Noah, the eighth person...bringing the flood upon the world of the ungodly....'

"For the unbiased reader there cannot be any doubt that Moses and other inspired writers mentioned above, including our Lord Himself, regarded the Deluge as a universal flood and a great historical fact. To deny this means to question the infallibility of the Bible and that of Christ Himself."[8]

CHAPTER TEN

The World in Which We Live

The Dead Sea is part of an enormous rift in the earth's crust stretching from the Ararat mountains in northeastern Turkey to Johannesburg in South Africa, nearly 4,500 miles (left). These kinds of rifts continued to develop after Noah and his family left the ark (right).

"For the anxious longing of the creation waits eagerly for the revealing of the sons of God."[1]

All around us we can see the effects of the original fall and of the Great Flood of Noah—on the face of the earth, in the animal kingdom, and among individuals and nations. The same kinds of things that happened in universal, cataclysmic proportions immediately before and during the flood occur around the world in smaller proportions. Volcanos erupt, forming new mountains, making islands disappear. Floods inundate low-lying areas, depositing rich silt and soil which can be used in subsequent years for fertile agriculture lands. Earthquakes devastate cities and open long fissures in the earth's crust. One rift is so long it reaches from the mountains of Ararat, through the Dead Sea, and the length of Africa, all the way to Johannesburg in South Africa. A lava flow obliterates all life in its path, leaving a landscape so barren it looks like the surface of a lifeless planet. The apostle Paul spoke truly when he said that the whole creation groans in anticipation of the liberation of the "sons of God."

But at the same time, the creation still points to the almighty, loving, and intelligent Creator and Sustainer. "The heavens are telling of the glory of God; and their expanse is declaring the work of His hands. Day to day pours forth speech, and night to night reveals knowledge. There is no speech, nor are there words; their voice is not heard. Their line has gone out through all the earth, and their utterances to the end of the world. In them He has placed a tent for the sun, which is as a bridegroom coming out of his chamber; it rejoices as a strong man to run his course. Its rising is from one end of the heavens, and its circuit to the other end of them; and there is nothing hidden from its heat."[2]

In this book we have seen the marvelous works of God in creation, His sustaining power, and His judgment against the wickedness of mankind. We have examined some theories of those who reject belief in God. These theories of the origin and development of life do not fit the evidence, or logic, or the Word of God.

The book of Job is the oldest book of the Bible. Its story may be older than that of Moses or even Abraham. Job suffered for his faith and ultimately was blessed by God.

In our first chapter we discussed the philosophical background to the scientific rejection of belief in God, the supernatural, and creation. We saw that men rejected God first, and then sought to find support for their rejection in the world around them.

In chapter two we reviewed the atheistic theories concerning the origin of the universe. We saw that most such theories arise from a rejection of God rather than from examining the evidence of the universe itself. We then saw that it makes more sense, both scientifically and logically, to believe that the universe, which is real, did have a beginning and that beginning was caused by an intelligent, all-powerful Creator outside the universe itself.

Chapter three gave us insight into the attributes of God on the basis of the design we see reflected in the universe. We reviewed some arguments people raise against design in the universe.

The origin of life was the subject of chapter four. We explored some of the nontheistic ideas concerning the origin of life as we know it on earth. We saw that atheistic scientists postulate that life arose spontaneously and randomly, life that was at first very simple and then more complex. When we looked at the evidence, however, the only logical theory as to the origin of life was that it was the deliberate creation of God.

156

Charles Darwin and his general theory of evolution (modified and expanded today) were the subjects of chapter five. The general theory of evolution is that simpler forms of life developed gradually, over an extremely long period of time, into more complex forms of life. Plants developed into invertebrates, invertebrates into vertebrates, amphibians into reptiles, and reptiles into warm-blooded animals. Looking at the scientific evidence from a biblical perspective, however, we saw the illogical presuppositions of evolution. We saw that both science and the Bible point toward God as the Creator of all basic life forms, from which specialized or adaptive family members developed.

A Sumerian clay cylinder relief (ca. 2100-1900 B.C.) of the moon goddess. Worship of the sun and moon is mentioned, but condemned, in the book of Job.

Chapter six concerned the testimony of the fossil record. Evolutionists insist that the lower strata, which contain simple life forms, represent the oldest and most primitive life on earth. The highest strata are said to represent the youngest and most complex life on earth. Such an interpretation fits the evolutionary hypothesis that life developed from simple to complex. The fossil record itself, however, does not fit the evolutionary plan. We saw that the sequence of strata could be accounted for more reasonably by postulating a universal and cataclysmic flood, the great flood of Noah's time, which would have deposited the marine (simple) layers of life first, then quickly the other life forms, accounting for the mass "graves" of fossilized bones found scattered around the world.

In chapter seven we specifically discussed mankind. Did we human beings develop "late" in the geological time line, from simpler life forms, with our immediate ancestors also being the ancestors of today's primates—monkeys, apes, and lemurs? Evolutionists believe that is so. It is in line with their presuppositions that humans are no more than sophisticated animals, the latest edition in a long and slow evolutionary process that was begun and is maintained by nonintelligent chance.

Our discussions and observations in chapter eight helped us to understand how the great flood fits into the biblical account and the physical record (especially the fossils) in the earth around us. We discussed the nontheistic scientific bias toward uniformitarianism rather than catastrophism. We showed that the catastrophic theory of the shaping of our modern earth and its life is in harmony with the evidence and the Bible.

Finally, chapter nine gave us information on Noah, the ark, and the flood that inundated the entire earth, changing its face forever. We saw that the flood had a theological as well as a physical aspect. It was God's judgment against sinful humanity. We also saw that Noah, a man of faith, was saved, along with his family and representative animals, as a picture ("type") of God's grace and forgiveness.

Job also mentions ostriches (Job 39:13-18) and lions (Job 38:39-41). Neither animal lives in the Middle East today.

In this final chapter we will reflect on some of the wonderful aspects of creation and protection by our Creator, God. We will see the mighty power of God as described by the Bible. We will see that human beings were created by God for a spiritual purpose not given to any other earthly creation. Finally, we will glimpse the coming cataclysm which, like the flood of Noah, will be the pronouncement of a holy God against sinfulness. And, most important, we will see how to escape that horrible catastrophe through faith in the Lord Jesus Christ.

God's Creation

The universe around us, the earth beneath, the life, both plant and animal, with which we are surrounded, all testify to creation by God. There is order, design, purposefulness, beauty and complexity in the world around us. Blind force could never create a flower. Instinct could never explain the love of parents for their children. Randomness could never produce true order. Bernard Ramm notes:

"The first feature of the biblical view of Nature is that it is a very frank *creationism. God is the Almighty Creator of heaven and earth.* Therefore, Nature exists fundamentally for spiritual purposes, and is capable of *teleological* explanation. This frank creationism is found in both Testaments. It is a theme that is constantly on the lips of the prophets.

To the Hebrew prophet Nature was not neutral in regard to the existence of God. Nature was a glorious tribute to the power, majesty, wisdom, splendour and benevolence of God. No biblical writer would concur with Pascal and Kierkegaard that God was secretly present in his works. To the biblical writers Nature is theistically committed."[3]

The Scriptures abound with testimony to the creative power of God. For example, in the book of Job we find repeated reference to the creation by God, and God Himself is quoted extensively concerning His creative power. Job talks of God's creation and even acknowledges the Lord's power to cause the great flood:

Right: Snow and ice, spoken of in Job, are now rare in the Middle East.
Below: A beautifully preserved skull from one of the earliest layers of the occupation of Jericho.

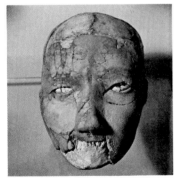

"With Him are wisdom and might; to Him belong counsel and understanding. Behold, He tears down, and it cannot be rebuilt; He imprisons a man, and there can be no release. Behold, He restrains the waters, and they dry up; and He sends them out, and they inundate the earth."[4]

Job continues in a later conversation, saying:

"He stretches out the north over empty space, and hangs the earth on nothing. He wraps up the waters in His clouds; and the cloud does not burst under them. He obscures the face of the full moon, and spreads His cloud over it. He has inscribed a circle on the surface of the waters, at the boundary of light and darkness. The pillars of heaven tremble, and are amazed at His rebuke. He quieted the sea with His power, and by His understanding. He shattered Rahab. By His breath the heavens are cleared; His hand has pierced the fleeing serpent."[5]

Finally, in the latter chapters of Job, the Lord God Himself declared His almighty power in creating the world and everything in it:

"Then the Lord answered Job out of the whirlwind and said, 'Who is this that darkens counsel by words without knowledge? Now gird up your loins like a man, and I will ask you, and you instruct me! Where were you when I laid the foundation of the earth! Tell Me, if you have understanding, who set its measurements, since you know? Or who stretched the line upon it? On what were its bases sunk? Or who laid its cornerstone, when the morning stars sang together, and all the sons of God shouted for joy? Or who enclosed the sea with doors, when, bursting forth, it went out from the womb; when I made a cloud its garment, and thick darkness its swaddling band, and I placed boundaries on it, and I set a bolt and doors, and I said, "Thus far you shall come, but no farther; and here shall your proud waves stop?" Have you ever in your life commanded the morning, and caused the dawn to know its place; that it might take hold of the ends of the earth, and the wicked be shaken out of it?'"[6]

Here in the mighty proclamations of the Lord God we see the majesty and power of His creation. The universe is not a senseless jumble of mass and energy. The solar system is not a chance relationship among pieces of matter in space. The earth is not a product of random "nature," giving only the illusion of order, design, and purpose. Plant and animal life is not a mass of evolutionary mistakes and "good tries," on the way to something better through directionless trial and error. And human life is not just a chemical process trapped in matter. With God as Creator, we are not alone. Richard Purtill comments:

"Thus, in the upshot, a universe without God is also a universe without meaning, a universe in which reason is not to be trusted, the moral law has no force, the hope of happiness is doomed to frustration. If we were forced to accept such a universe we would have to make the best of it we could, as the Epicureans, and the Sceptics, too, in their own way, tried to do. But what can force us to such a view? No external compulsion, for too many men of all kinds reject the view. Not reason, for the view denies its validity. Not morality, for the view denies any force to morality. Not hope of happiness, for the view rejects this hope. Thus there can be *no* reasons for accepting the view that the universe is meaningless, and there are excellent reasons for accepting the theistic view, which makes sense of the intelligibility of the universe, the felt force of the moral law, and our intimations of happiness. The difficulties of accepting and understanding the theistic view may be formidable, but the difficulties of rejecting it are insurmountable. To this conclusion reason leads us, and we can reject it only by rejecting reason."[7]

The God of all creation is One in whom we can have perfect confidence. Certainly He deserves our praise for His mighty works of creation.

God's Protection

The same God who created everything also preserves, sustains, and protects His creation. The same section of Job chronicles God's work of control over the creation He has made:

"Can you bind the chains of the Pleiades, or loose the cords of Orion? Can you lead forth a constellation in its season, and guide the Bear with her satellites? Do you know the ordinances of the heavens, or fix their rule over the earth? Can you lift up your voice to the clouds, so that an abundance of water may cover you? Can you send forth lightnings that they may go and say to you, 'Here we are'? Who has put wisdom in the innermost being, or has given understanding to the mind? Who can count the clouds by wisdom, or tip the water jars of the heavens, when the dust hardens into a mass, and the clods stick together?'"[8]

Everywhere in the creation we see the protective hand of God. Although it is true that the world suffers from the effects of the fall adn the flood, God's handiwork is still in evidence. God has not abandoned His creation. On the contrary, if it were not for His continual preservation of the world, nothing could continue to exist. Psalm 36:6 reminds us, "O Lord, Thou preservest man and beast." The apostle Paul, in Acts 17, declared that in God "we live and move and exist" (v. 28). Jesus Christ is described by Paul as the sustainer of the universe. "He is before all things, and in Him all things hold together."

Bernard Ramm reminds us:

"The biblical view of Nature also clearly maintains that *the universe is maintained by the providence of God.* Biblical theism is unfriendly to deism and pantheism. It refuses to identify God with His works and it refuses to bar God from His works. God is *world-ground* of all things to biblical theism, and He sustains not only the physical order but the moral and spiritual orders too. The providence of God is deeper than critics of biblical supernaturalism realize. God's providence is His working all things to their destined goal. In cooperation with the redemption of God it forms the basis of the Christian philosophy of history. In that God works through the natural and human, providence applies to nature. The possibility of miracles, and the possibility of answered prayer, are deeply involved in the biblical doctrine of providence. And in turn providence is deeply involved with the biblical doctrine of nature and God's relation to His creation. The God of the Bible is not manacled to causal laws, nor is He a prisoner in His own creation. The liberal and neoorthodox doctrine of the providence of God and the relationship of God to nature is extremely faulty and anti-biblical. Biblical theism with its unalloyed creationism will not tolerate the metaphysics of religious modernism or of neo-orthodoxy. The providence of God demands the freedom of God in nature. The Bible is just as frank about its providence as it is about its creationism."[10]

Because of the protective and preserving power of God, Noah and we, his descendants, can trust God's promise, signed with the rainbow, that He will never again destroy life as we know it by flood. (As we shall see soon, however, judgment will come by fire.) The universe is God's creation. Who else has better authority by which to control and direct it?

God's Power

Nothing is too hard for the Creator of the universe. In another of our books, we put it this way:

"When we say that God is all-powerful, we mean that anything which is capable of being done, God can do. He cannot do the logically or intrinsically impossible. The Christian theologian James Oliver Buswell, Jr., writes,

> ...omnipotence does not mean that God can do anything, but it does mean that He can do with power anything that power can do. He has all the power that is or could be.

Can God make two plus two equal six? This is a question which is frequently asked by skeptics and by children. We reply by asking how much power it would take to bring about this result. The absurdity of the question is not too difficult to see. Would the power

The enormous power of waves is demonstrated throughout the world. Imagine the force of water and waves in a worldwide flood!

of a ton of dynamite make two plus two equal six? or the power of an atom bomb? or of a hydrogen bomb? When these questions are asked it is readily seen that the truth of the multiplication tables is not in the realm of power. Power has nothing to do with it. When we assert that God is omnipotent, we are talking about power (James Oliver Buswell, *A Systematic Theology of the Christian Religion,* Grand Rapids, MI: Zondervan Publishing House, 1962, pp. 63,64)."[11]

So then, with all power, the God of the universe creates, sustains, and acts.

With His power He formed the world. Genesis 1 declares that "God said"—and creation happened. Such is the power of God.

With His power He sustains the world. Psalm 29 declares that the voice of God "breaks the cedars" and "makes Lebanon skip like a calf." This is the power with which He sustains His creation.

With His power He acts on behalf of His creation. Psalm 33 talks of the overriding power of God's plans: "The Lord nullifies the counsel of nations; He frustrates the plans of the peoples. The counsel of the Lord stands forever, the plans of His heart from generation to generation."[12]

Henry Morris acknowledges the power of God, noting other Scripture verses in substantiation of it:

An artist's rendition of the idolatry and false worship associated with the Tower of Babel.

"The great Designer who created this wonderful world can be none other than the God of the Bible—omnipotent, omnipresent, omniscient, holy—yet also personal, loving, and gracious. The Cause of all the phenomena of the universe must encompass at least all their own characteristics. 'He that planted the ear, shall he not hear? He that formed the eye, shall he not see?...He that teacheth man knowledge, shall he not know?' (Psalm 94:9-10).

"The finely-balanced structure of the earth's hydrosphere, atmosphere, and lithosphere are stressed in the rhetorical question of Isaiah 40:12: 'Who hath measured the waters in the hollow of his hand, and meted out heaven with the span, and comprehended the dust of the earth in a measure, and weighed the mountains in scales, and the hills in a balance?'

"As if in answer, the prophet replies by stressing God's omnipotence and omniscience: 'Lift up your eyes on high, and behold who hath created these things, that bringeth out their host by number: he calleth them all by names by the greatness of his might, for that he is strong in power; not one faileth' (40:26).

"The tremendous evidence of design and order in nature encourages us to testify with the Psalmist: 'O Lord, how manifold are thy works! In wisdom hast thou made them all: the earth is full of thy riches' (Psalm 104:24)."[13]

We are convinced that the power of God is evident in the universe and that, in fact, the existence of the universe itself is testimony to God's wisdom, benevolence, and justice.

Why Are We Here?

Just a few pages ago, we quoted the book of Job for its insights on God's creating the universe. Now we refer to that book again to point out that humans are conscious, thinking, and worshiping beings because of God's creative act. In Job 38:36, the Lord asks, rhetorically, "Who has put wisdom in the innermost being, or has given understanding to the mind?" As we discussed in more depth in chapter seven, human life is more than a mass of chemicals in reaction. Human thought is not based on random impulses that merely imitate order and intelligence. Each of us really is a *personal being*, made in God's image. We are the only part of the earth's creation that can worship Him. Only we have the capability for rational thought. The first responsibility God gave to the first man was to "name" the animals as they were brought before him by God's direction. Only human beings have inclination to

Mountain ranges were flattened and new mountain ranges were thrust up by the enormous forces unleashed through the flood

name the life we see around us. (Even today, nontheistic scientists spend thousands of hours classifying and "naming" every living and non-living thing they can observe.)

Harris notes the purpose for which human beings were created:

"...the Old Testament recognizes a kinship between God and men that is unique in this world. It is dependent upon the kinship established by the original creation of man in the divine image. A further point of value is that heavenly beings are also called "sons of God" in the book of Job (1:6, 2:1, 38:7). Thus our relation of sonship to God and the stamp of the image of God upon us is similar to that of the angels. Like them we are spiritual, rational, moral beings. But they do not have our bodily form except when sent to speak to men. Clearly the image of God in man as presented in the Old Testament presumes a nonmaterial nature with spiritual attributes—in short, a soul."[14]

But something happened after humankind was created. The first human beings, Adam and Eve of Genesis, deliberately disobeyed their Creator and broke the bond of fellowship and worship that had existed before that. From that point on, all creation was marred by their sin. Romans 5:12 declares that sin entered into the world through one man—Adam—and death from sin. By the time of Noah (Scripture does not specifically date Noah's time), humanity was so thoroughly evil that

God's solution was a judgment that had catastrophic consequence for the earth, its plants and animals, and the entire human race. God destroyed all people except for Noah and his family by means of the great flood, which we discussed at length in other chapters. Noah himself was not perfect; he suffered the effects of Adam's sin just as every other descendant of Adam had. But Noah had faith. God saved Noah, warning him and instructing him to build the ark.

Since Noah's time there have been good persons and bad persons. People of faith and people who mocked God. Nations have served the Lord, and nations have risen against the Lord's people. (In volume

Right: The Cape Verde Islands may be the tops of mountains which were once above water and inhabited.
Below: Plato records the destruction by tidal wave of an ancient land, Atlantis. (Whether such a place actually existed or was mythological is unknown.)

three we will discuss the history of the Bible and God's people.) Never since has the earth seen destruction such as was wrought by the great flood. But the day will come when further judgment and calamities will come on the whole earth. This judgment, the final judgment, will be on all who reject the truth of God. Harris summarizes the relationship of man with God:

"As has been shown above, the Old Testament is abundantly clear that man is not a machine, not a mere animal, but a child of God.... Man lives in constant confrontation with God, standing in God's love or judgment. God throughout the Old Testament seeks fellowship with man as He does with no other creature of this earth. Man is more akin to the angels than to the clod."[15]

That constant confrontation will have its final match during the cataclysm described by the apostle Peter (2 Peter 3). Peter first describes the earth and its inhabitants just before the judgment. His description reminds us of the world we see around us today:

"Know this first of all, that in the last days mockers will come with their mocking, following after their own lusts, and saying, 'Where is the promise of His coming? For ever since the fathers fell asleep, all continues just as it was from the beginning of creation.' For when they maintain this, it escapes their notice that by the word of God the

heavens existed long ago and the earth was formed out of water and by water, through which the world at that time was destroyed, being flooded with water."[16]

According to Jesus and the apostles, the great flood was a prototype of the final judgment awaiting the present world. Rehwinkel notes the similarities between the world of Noah and today:

"As in the days of Noah, so the world today has reached an unprecedented stage of material and technical progress. There never was a time in the history of man when physical advantages, comforts, luxuries, and leisure were so widely distributed as in our age. We harnessed the forces of nature and have compelled them to do our

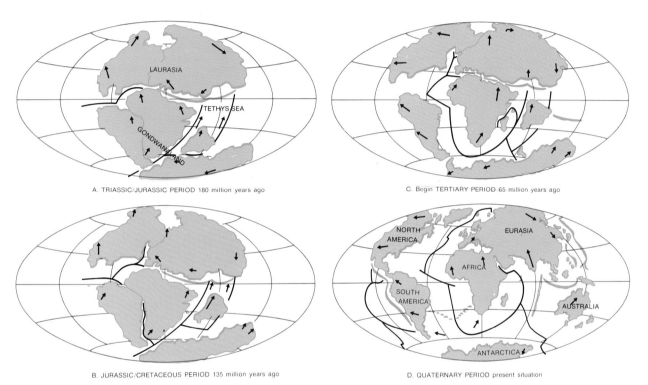

A. TRIASSIC/JURASSIC PERIOD 180 million years ago

C. Begin TERTIARY PERIOD 65 million years ago

B. JURASSIC/CRETACEOUS PERIOD 135 million years ago

D. QUATERNARY PERIOD present situation

Above: a reconstruction of the "continental drift" according to the evolution model. (A) The original continent, Pangaea, begins to divide; the Tethys Sea was a shallow sea between Africa and Asia. (B) The rifts have widened; India, separated from Antarctica-Australia, moves in the direction of Asia. (C) The continents have almost reached their present locations. (D) The present situation; the Americas are linked by Central America; India has attached itself to Asia (the "collision" formed the Himalayas).

bidding....Superstition, ignorance, and illiteracy are rapidly disappearing. Human suffering is being alleviated, life is prolonged, and men even speak of the time when death will be abolished.

"But there is a counterpart to all this material progress. As of the first generation, so must it be said of the great masses today that they are flesh. They are no longer governed or guided by the Spirit of God. Our age is an age of worldliness, or carnal-mindedness, and secularism; violence and wickedness abound. The philosophy of the average man is decidedly a this-world philosophy....

"Such is a picture of the world today. In the chapter which gives the reasons why God brought the world-wide flood upon the first world, we read: 'And God saw that the wickedness of man was great in the earth, and that every imagination of the thoughts of his heart was only evil continually....The earth also was corrupt before God, and the earth was filled with violence. And God looked upon the earth, and, behold, it was corrupt, for all flesh had corrupted his way upon the earth' (Gen. 6:5, 11-12).

"This description most certainly fits our own generation. The world is

Above: A painting from the Middle Ages of Noah and the ark.

ripening fast for its final judgment. It would be well therefore that we heed the warning of Peter when he says: 'The Lord is not slack concerning His promise as some men count slackness; but is long-suffering to us-ward, not willing that any should perish, but that all should come to repentance. But the Day of the Lord shall come as a thief in the night, in the which the heavens shall pass away with a great noise and the elements shall melt with fervent heat, the earth also and the works that are therein shall be burned up. Seeing, then, that all these things shall be dissolved, what manner of persons ought ye to be in all holy conversation and godliness, looking for and hasting unto the coming of the day of God, wherein the heavens, being on fire, shall be dissolved and the elements shall melt with fervent heat! Nevertheless, we, according to his promise, look for new heavens and a new earth wherein dwelleth righteousness. Wherefore, beloved, seeing that ye look for such things, be diligent that ye may be found of Him in peace, without spot and blameless' (2 Pet. 3:9-14)."[17]

We, too, can be confident that we are in Him, "in peace, without spot and blameless." We, too, can be part of "Noah's family," and know that God will rescue us from the coming judgment.

Above: The Bible foretells future judgment and destruction by God against sinful mankind. Only those who have trusted in the blood of Jesus Christ for salvation will be spared. "When these things begin to take place, stand up and lift up your heads, because your redemption is drawing near" (Luke 21:28).

If you do not know for sure that you are a Christian, and if you have never accepted Jesus Christ as your Lord and Savior, you need to study carefully the material below. Then act on it, and know that you belong to the Creator of heaven and earth.

Notes

Chapter 1

1. *Encyclopaedia Britannica.* Chicago, IL: Encyclopaedia Britannica Inc., 1978, *Macropaedia,* vol. 7, p. 852.
2. Bernard Ramm, *The Christian View of Science and Scripture.* Grand Rapids, MI: William B. Eerdmans Publishing Company, 1954, p. 25.
3. Stillman Drake, *Galileo.* New York: Hill and Wang, 1980, p. 59.
4. For an analysis and critique of Marxism, see our *Understanding Secular Religions,* San Bernardino, CA: Here's Life Publishers, 1982.
5. Hebrews 11:1, 3.
6. 1 Corinthians 15:1-3.
7. 1 Corinthians 15:17.
8. Matthew 28:5, 6.
9. Acts 2:22, 32; italics ours.
10. 2 Peter 1:16.
11. Acts 17:2, 3; italics ours.
12. Acts 17:16.
13. Acts 17:17; italics ours.
14. Acts 17:22-31.
15. Acts 17:24, 25.
16. Hebrews 1:3.
17. Colossians 1:15-17.
18. Robert Jastrow, *God and the Astronomers.* New York: W. W. Norton and Company, Inc., 1978, p. 113.
19. Jastrow, *Astronomers,* pp. 115, 116.

Chapter 2

1. Lewis Spence, *An Encyclopaedia of Occultism.* Secaucus, NJ: The Citadel Press, 1960, p. 42.
2. George O. Abell, "The Mars Effect," *Psychology Today,* July 1982, p. 8.
3. Michael Van Buskirk, *Astrology: Revival in the Cosmic Garden.* Costa Mesa, CA: Christian Apologetics: Research and Information Service—CARIS, 1978, p. 3.
4. Deuteronomy 18:9-12 KJV; italics ours.
5. Deuteronomy 17:2-5; italics ours.
6. Daniel 1:20 KJV; italics ours.
7. Isaiah 44:24, 25; italics ours.
8. Isaiah 47:13-15; italics ours.
9. Abell, "Mars Effect," p. 8.
10. Josh McDowell and Don Stewart, *Understanding the Occult.* San Bernardino, CA: Here's Life Publishers, 1982, pp. 26-30.
11. Van Buskirk, *Astrology,* pp. 4-9.
12. Van Buskirk, *Astrology,* p. 4.
13. McDowell and Stewart, *Occult,* p. 28.
14. Abell, "Mars Effect," p. 9.
15. Van Buskirk, *Astrology,* p. 8.
16. Kenneth Boa, *Cults, World Religions, and You.* Wheaton, IL: Victor Books, 1977, pp. 124, 125.
17. McDowell and Stewart, *Occult,* p. 27.
18. Bernard Ramm, *The Christian View of Science and Scripture.* Grand Rapids, MI: William B. Eerdmans Publishing Company, 1954, pp. 23, 24.
19. Jack Wood Sears, *Conflict and Harmony in Science and the Bible,* Grand Rapids, MI: Baker Book House, 1969, pp. 22, 23.
20. Richard Purtill, *Reason to Believe.* Grand Rapids, MI: William B. Eerdmans Publishing Company, 1974, pp. 81, 82.
21. Edwin A. Abbott, *Flatland.* New York: Dover Publications, 1952, p. 102.
22. Josh McDowell and Don Stewart, *Understanding Non-Christian Religions.* San Bernardino, CA: Here's Life Publishers, 1982.

23. Henry M. Morris, *The Bible and Modern Science*. Chicago, IL: Moody Press, 1951, 1968, pp. 11-13.
24. E. M. Blaiklock, ed., *Why I Am Still a Christian*. Grand Rapids, MI: Zondervan Publishing House, 1971, pp. 12, 13.

Chapter 3

1. Henry M. Morris, *The Remarkable Birth of Planet Earth*. Minneapolis, MN: Bethany Fellowship, Inc., 1972, p. 5.
2. Psalm 8:3-6.
3. Romans 8:19-22.
4. Acts 17:24, 25.
5. Isaiah 44:24.
6. Job 38:4-11.
7. James H. Jauncey, *Science Returns to God*. Grand Rapids, MI: Zondervan Publishing House, 1971, p. 19.
8. The discovery that matter and energy are interconvertible means that matter can disappear if an equivalent amount of energy appears, and vice-versa. Albert Einstein expressed the equivalence of matter and energy in a now famous equation, $E = mc^2$, where E is energy, m is the mass of equivalent matter, and c is the velocity of light.
9. Peter W. Stoner, *Science Speaks*. Chicago, IL: Moody Press, 1969, pp. 25, 26.
10. Stoner, *Science Speaks*, pp. 114, 115.

Chapter 4

1. Genesis 1:26, 27.
2. Harry Rimmer, *The Harmony of Science and Scripture*. Grand Rapids, MI: William B. Eerdmans Publishing Company, 1936, p. 125.
3. Kingsley Mortimer, "An Anatomist's Testimony," in Blaiklock, *Why I Am Still a Christian*, pp. 138, 139.
4. Genesis 1:11, 12.
5. Bernard Ramm, *The Christian View of Science and Scripture*. Grand Rapids, MI: William B. Eerdmans Publishing Company, 1954, p. 181.
6. Henry M. Morris. *The Remarkable Birth of Planet Earth*. Minneapolis, MN: Bethany Fellowship, Inc., 1972, pp. 34, 35.
7. L. Duane Thurman, *How to Think about Evolution*. Downers Grove, IL: Inter-Varsity Press, 1978, pp. 99, 100.
8. Ramm, *Christian View*, pp. 181, 182.
9. Bolton Davidheiser, *Evolution and Christian Faith*. Nutley, NJ: The Presbyterian and Reformed Publishing Company, 1969, p. 220.
10. Davidheiser, *Evolution*, p. 221.
11. Davidheiser, *Evolution*, p. 221, 222.
12. Davidheiser, *Evolution*, p. 222.
13. Ramm, *Christian View*, p. 183.
14. Thurman, *Evolution*, p. 54.

Chapter 5

1. Bolton Davidheiser, *Evolution and Christian Faith*. Nutley, NJ: The Presbyterian and Reformed Publishing Company, 1969, p. 67 (quoting Darwin's autobiography).
2. This controverted the biblical assertion of a universal flood, among other theories.
3. Davidheiser, *Evolution*, p. 61.
4. Adapted from John W. Klotz, *Genes, Genesis, and Evolution*. St. Louis: Concordia Publishing House, 1955, 1970, pp. 34, 35.
5. Klotz, *Genes*, p. 34.
6. Klotz, *Genes*, pp. 38, 39.
7. L. Duane Thurman, *How to Think About Evolution*. Downers Grove, IL: Inter-Varsity Press, 1978, pp. 90, 91.
8. Thurman, *Evolution*, p. 91.
9. Thurman, *Evolution*, pp. 45, 46.
10. Duane T. Gish, *Evolution: The Fossils Say No*. San Diego, CA: Creation-Life Publishers, 1978, p. 50.
11. Gish, *Evolution*, pp. 38, 39.
12. Klotz, *Genes*, pp. 72, 73.

13. Thurman, *Evolution*, pp. 94, 95.

14. Thurman, *Evolution*, p. 112.

Chapter 6

1. John W. Klotz, *Genes, Genesis, and Evolution*. St. Louis, MO: Concordia Publishing House, 1955, 1970, p. 185.

2. Henry M. Morris, *The Remarkable Birth of Planet Earth*. Minneapolis, MN: Bethany Fellowship, Inc., 1972, p. 22.

3. Klotz, *Genes*, pp. 203, 204.

4. *Klotz, Genes, p. 204.*

5. *Morris, Planet Earth, p. 30.*

6. J. Kerby Anderson and Harold G. Coffin, *Fossils in Focus*. Grand Rapids, MI: Zondervan Publishing House, 1977, p. 44.

7. Bolton Davidheiser, *Evolution and Christian Faith*. Nutley, NJ: The Presbyterian and Reformed Publishing Company, 1969, p. 283.

8. Anderson and Coffin, *Fossils*, p. 27.

9. Duane T. Gish, *Evolution: The Fossils Say No*. San Diego, CA: Creation-Life Publishers, 1978, p. 64.

10. Gish, *Evolution*, p. 65.

11. Anderson and Coffin, *Fossils*, pp. 53, 54.

12. Gish, *Evolution*, p. 84.

13. Anderson and Coffin, *Fossils*, pp. 55, 57.

14. Gish, *Evolution*, pp. 62, 63.

15. Morris, *Planet Earth*, p. 27.

16. L. Duane Thurman, *How to Think About Evolution*. Downers Grove, IL: Inter-Varsity Press, 1978, pp. 106, 107.

17. Anderson and Coffin, *Fossils*, p. 72.

18. Morris, *Planet Earth*, p. 30.

Chapter 7

1. A.E. Wilder-Smith, *Man's Origin, Man's Destiny*. Minneapolis, MN: Bethany Fellowship, Inc., 1968, pp. 111, 112.

2. R. Allen Killen, "Anthropology," *Wycliffe Bible Encyclopedia*, Vol. 1. Chicago, IL: Moody Press, p. 101.

3. Russell L. Mixter, *Evolution and Christian Thought Today*. Grand Rapids, MI: William B. Eerdmans Publishing Company, 1959, p. 181.

4. Genesis 2:21-23.

5. Morris, *The Remarkable Birth of Planet Earth*, pp. 44, 45.

6. R. Laird Harris, *Man—God's Eternal Creation*. Chicago, IL: Moody Press, 1971, p. 51.

7. Sir Julian Huxley, quoted in Arthur Koestler's *The Ghost in the Machine*. London, England: Hutchinson, 1967, p. 297.

8. Harris, *Man*, pp. 8, 9.

9. Quoted in Arthur Custance, *Evolution or Creation*. Grand Rapids, MI: Zondervan Publishing House, 1976, p. 215.

10. John W. Klotz, *Genes, Genesis, and Evolution*. St. Louis: Concordia Publishing House, 1955, p. 384.

11. Duane T. Gish. *Evolution: The Fossils Say No*. San Diego, CA: Creation-Life Publishers, 1978, p. 114.

12. Gish, *Evolution*, p. 128.

13. Quoted in Bolton Davidheiser, *Evolution and Christian Faith*. Nutley, NJ: The Presbyterian and Reformed Publishing Company, 1969, p. 347.

14. Davidheiser, *Evolution*, p. 348.

15. Gish, *Evolution*, pp. 120, 121.

16. Wilder-Smith, *Man's Origin*, p. 133.

17. Davidheiser, *Evolution*, p. 332.

18. Mixter, *Christian Thought*, pp. 176, 177.

19. Klotz, *Genes*, p. 387.

20. Gish, *Evolution*, p. 139.

21. Harris, *Man*, p. 66.

22. Harris, *Man*, p. 71.

Chapter 8

1. Henry Morris, ed., *Scientific Creationism*. San Diego, CA: Creation-Life Publishers, 1974, p. 91.
2. *Encyclopaedia Britannica*. Chicago, IL: Encyclopaedia Britannica, Inc., 1979, *Macropaedia*, vol. 18, p. 859.
3. Genesis 7:11-24.
4. John C. Whitcomb, "Flood," *Wycliffe Bible Encyclopaedia*, Vol. 1, p. 614.
5. Morris, *Scientific Creationism*, p. 97.
6. Morris, *Scientific Creationism*, pp. 112, 113.
7. Morris, *Scientific Creationism*, p. 115.
8. Morris, *Scientific Creationism*, p. 112.

Chapter 9

1. Alfred M. Rehwinkel, *The Flood*. St. Louis, MO: Concordia Publishing House, 1951, pp. 153, 154.
2. Bernard Ramm, *The Christian View of Science and Scripture*. Grand Rapids, MI: William B. Eerdmans Publishing Company, 1954, p. 158.
3. Frederick Filby, *The Flood Reconsidered*. Grand Rapids, MI: Zondervan Publishing House, 1970, p. 56.
4. Rehwinkel, *Flood*, p. 164.
5. Exodus 2:3, 5.
6. Ramm, *Christian View*, p. 157.
7. Filby, *Flood*, p. 92.
8. Rehwinkel, *Flood*, pp. 94, 95.

Chapter 10

1. Romans 8:19.
2. Psalm 19:1-6.
3. Bernard Ramm. *The Christian View of Science and Scripture*. Grand Rapids, MI: William B. Eerdmans Publishing Company, 1954, p. 56.
4. Job 12:13-15.
5. Job 26:7-13.
6. Job 38:1-13.
7. Richard Purtill, *Reason to Believe*. Grand Rapids, MI: William B. Eerdmans Publishing Company, 1974, pp. 111, 112.
8. Job 38:31-38.
9. Colossians 1:17.
10. Ramm, *Christian View*, p. 57.
11. Josh McDowell and Don Stewart, *Understanding Secular Religions*, 1982, p. 36.
12. Psalm 33:10, 11.
13. Henry M. Morris, *The Remarkable Birth of Planet Earth*, Minneapolis, MN: Bethany Fellowship, Inc., 1972, pp. 11-12.
14. R. Laird Harris, *Man—God's Eternal Creation*. Chicago, IL: Moody Press, 1971, p. 21.
15. Harris, *Man*, pp. 162, 163.
16. 2 Peter 3:3-6.
17. Alfred M. Rehwinkel, *The Flood*. St. Louis, MO: Concordia Publishing House, 1951, pp. 343-350.

Recommended Reading

Anderson, J. Kerby and Harold G. Coffin, *Fossils in Focus*, Grand Rapids, MI: Zondervan Publishing House, 1977.

Andrews, E.H., *God, Science and Evolution*, Hertfordshire, England: Evangelical Press, 1980.

Blaiklock, E.M., ed., *Why I Am Still a Christian*, Grand Rapids, MI: Zondervan Publishing House, 1971.

Custance, Arthur C., *Evolution or Creation?*, Grand Rapids, MI: Zondervan Publishing House, 1976.

—————, *The Flood: Local or Global?*, Grand Rapids, MI: Zondervan Publishing House, 1979.

Davidheiser, Bolton, *Evolution and Christian Faith*, Nutley, NJ: Presbyterian and Reformed Publishing Company, 1969.

Filby, Frederick A., *The Flood Reconsidered*, Grand Rapids, MI: Zondervan Publishing House, 1970.

Gish, Duane T., *Evolution: The Fossils Say No!*, San Diego, CA: Creation-Life Publishers, 1978.

Hall, Marshall and Sandra, *The Truth: God or Evolution?*, Grand Rapids, MI: Baker Books, 1974.

Harris, R. Laird, *Man—God's Eternal Creation*, Chicago, IL: Moody Press, 1971.

Jauncy, James H., *Science Returns to God*, Grand Rapids, MI: Zondervan Publishing House, 1971.

Klotz, John W., *Genes, Genesis and Evolution*, St. Louis, MO: Concordia Publishing House, 1955.

McDowell, Josh and Don Stewart, *Understanding Non-Christian Religions*, San Bernardino, CA: Here's Life Publishers, 1982.

—————, *Understanding Secular Religions*, San Bernardino, CA: Here's Life Publishers, 1982.

Mixter, Russell, ed., *Evolution and Christian Thought Today*, Grand Rapids, MI: William B. Eerdmans Publishing Company, 1959.

Morris, Henry M. and Duane T. Gish, eds., *The Battle for Creation*, San Diego, CA: Creation-Life Publishers, 1976.

Morris, Henry M., *The Bible and Modern Science*, Chicago, IL: Moody Press, 1968.

—————, *The Remarkable Birth of Planet Earth*, Minneapolis, MN: Bethany Fellowship, 1972.

—————, *Scientific Creationism*, San Diego, CA: Creation-Life Publishers, 1974.

—————, *The Twilight of Evolution*, Grand Rapids, MI: Baker Book House, 1963.

Nelson, Byron, *After Its Kind*, Minneapolis, MN: Bethany Fellowship, 1967.

Newman, Robert C. and Herman J. Eckelmann, Jr., *Genesis One and the Origin of the Earth*, Downers Grove, IL: InterVarsity Press, 1977.

Pfeiffer, Charles F. and Howard F. Vos and John Rea, eds., *Wycliffe Bible Encyclopedia*, Chicago, IL: Moody Press, 1975 (2 vols.).

Purtill, Richard, *Reason to Believe*, Grand Rapids, MI: William B. Eerdmans Publishing Company, 1974.

Ramm, Bernard, *The Christian View of Science and Scripture*, Grand Rapids, MI: William B. Eerdmans Publishing Company, 1954.

Rehwinkel, Alfred M., *The Flood in the Light of the Bible, Geology, and Archaeology*, St. Louis, MO: Concordia Publishing Company, 1951.

Rimmer, Harry, *The Harmony of Science and Scripture*, Grand Rapids, MI: William B. Eerdmans Publishing Company, 1936.

Rushdoony, Rousas John, *The Mythology of Science*, Nutley, NJ: The Craig Press, 1967.

Stoner, Peter W., *Science Speaks*, Chicago, IL: Moody Press, 1968.

Thurman, L. Duane, *How to Think About Evolution*, Downers Grove, IL: InterVarsity Press, 1978.

Wilder-Smith, A.E., *Man's Origin, Man's Destiny*, Minneapolis, MN: Bethany Fellowship, 1968.

Wilson, Clifford, *Monkeys Will Never Talk...or Will They?*, San Diego, CA: Creation-Life Publishers, 1978.

INDEX

A

Abbott, Edwin A. - 36
abiogenesis - 59
aborigines - 113
Abell, George E. - 27, 29
agnostic - 23
amber deposits - 88
amino acids - 58, 59, 62, 63
amphibians - 82, 95, 96, 134, 139, 157
Amun-Ra - 25
Anderson, J. Kerby - 91, 96, 97, 99, 102
animals - 151, 153
  cold-blooded - 152
  marine - 151
  on the ark - 151
  warm-blooded - 96, 134, 157
antisupernaturalism - 62
apologist - 12
Aquarius - 27
Aquinas, Thomas - 12, 13, 15
Aramburg - 120
Archaeopteryx - 97, 98
Aries - 27
ark - 148, 153, 158, 164
  Babylonian - 145
  biblical - 145, 149
  of Noah - 143, 149, 150
  of Utnapishtim - 149
Assurbanipal in Nineveh - 144
astrological charting - 27, 30
astrology - 25, 30-32
  ancient - 27
  contemporary - 27
  judicial - 27
  natural - 27
astronomy - 17, 18
atheist - 19, 20
atom - 54
atomic clocks - 101
Aton - 25
Australopithecus - 119, 121, 122
  africanus - 121
  habilis - 121
  robustus - 121

B

bacterium - 59
bats - 99
  Eocene - 99
  flying - 99
Beebe, William - 74
beginning - 18, 36, 38, 47, 48
biogenis, law of - 60
birds - 82, 96, 98
Blaiklock, E.M. - 39
Boule - 120
brachiopods - 93
British Museum - 144
Buswell, James Oliver, Jr. - 161

C

calcification - 88
Cambrian
  age - 94
  animals - 93
  fauna - 93
  fossil record - 91, 92
  layer - 92
  life forms - 94
  period - 92, 139
  strata - 93-95
Cancer - 27
Capricorn - 27
earbonate of lime - 87
catastrophism - 125, 127, 131, 135, 136, 158
catastrophist - 126, 127, 136
Caucasoid - 108
cell - 53, 54, 58, 59, 62, 65, 68, 78
  protosynthetic - 58
cell models - 63
ceremonial burial - 113
charmer - 28
chromosome - 54, 55
Clark - 64
coal - 89, 91, 136, 138
coal beds - 90
Coffin, Harold G. - 91, 96, 97, 99, 102
colloids - 63
Colossi of Memnon - 150
communism - 20
conflict - 15, 17, 32
consulter - 28
consinuous creation - 35
contradiction - 15, 16, 17, 21
Cook, H. - 116
Copernican theory - 15
Correns - 77
cosmic panspermia - 63
cosmology - 25, 27, 28, 32, 38, 46
  biblical - 28, 38
  scientific - 28, 38
cosmos - 27
craters - 14, 18
creation - 82, 83, 86
  Biblical account of... - 85
  God's... - 158, 160
creationism - 158, 161
Cretaceous Age - 100
Crossopterygian fish - 95

D

Darwin, Charles - 19, 20, 71-76, 78, 93, 113,
  119, 127, 157
Darwin, Eramus - 71
Darwinism - 72
data - 17, 18, 19
  astronomical - 18
  observed - 60

176

ILLUSTRATION CREDITS

The location of the illustrations is indicated by the following abbreviations and combinations thereof:

l. = left   r. = right   t. = top   b. = bottom   c. = center

The editors of this book have made every effort to trace the source of all illustrations. In some cases this was not possible. Claims should be submitted to the Publisher, who agrees to pay any fees due.

Afga Gevaert, Knudsen: 56
Heather Angel: 84, 95
Atlas Photo (Paris): 137 r. (Lubrano),
    48 t. (Charles Lenars)
Nico Baayens: 63 l. and r.
Museum Berger: 139
CNRS-Paris, Serge Koutchmy: 37
Bruce Coleman Limited: 46, 59 l., 74 r.,
    77 l. and r. (Hans Reinhard), 78 l., 79 r.,
    82 t.l. and b.l., 83, 85 r., 94 c. and r.,
    96 t., 98, 99 l., 105 r., 150 b., 158 l. and r.
Jack Dabner: 145 r., 148 l., 149, 163
Down House: 85 l.
Ellis-Sawyer: 67 b.
Fotomas Index: 30, 59 r., 70
Giraudon: 14 b.
Hama: 94 t.l.
Hansen Planetarium: 40, 50 t.
Hänssler Verlag: 136
Robert Harding: 104, 108 b.l. and t.l.,
    109 b.l. and t.l., 144 r.
M. Holfort Library: 31, 144, 146 l.
Institute of Geological Science: 42, 44 t. and
    b., 45 l., 64 t., 76 r., 87, 91 r., 93 l.,
    101 l. and r., 103 b., 140
Dr. D. James: 161
Kees Jansen: 18 l., 55 l., 76 l.
J. van de Kam: 92
Carl E. Koppeschaar: 13 r., 29 l., 32 t.,
    42 r., 61, 62, 78 r., 119 r. (via Kijk),
    122 l., 166
Kijk: 53
The Mansell Collection, London: 64 b., 110,
    118 l. and r., 147, 152,
Photo Melgär: 36 r.
Cees van de Meulen: 153
Prof. D. Murchison: 91 t.l.
Natuurhistorisch Museum, Maastricht,
    Netherlands, Jan van Eyk: 99 r.
National History Photographic Agency,
    J.W.C. Murray: 47 r.
NASA, Washington D.C.: 14 t., 60
A. van Nieuwenhuizen: 97 r.
Rob de Nooy: 57 l.
Pedina Litographica: 138 r.

Rapho Paris, Dr. Georg Gester: 24
Rijksmuseum voor Geschiedenis en
    Natuurwetenschappen, Leyden,
    Netherlands: 74 l.
Scala, Florence: 12, 13 l., 18 r., 21, 22, 51,
    54, 106, 108 r., 120 r., 130, 148 r., 151 b.,
    159 l., 164 l., 169
Dr. Joachim Scheven: 91 t.l., 100 r., 131 l.
    and r., 132, 139 l., 138 l. and r.
Cees Scholz: 79 l., 96 b.
Peter Schütte: 68
Science Museum, London: 48 b.
Skull: 119 t.l.
Fotoarchief Spaarnestad: 49, 111 l., 114 l.,
    115 r., 119 b.l.
Space Frontiers Ltd., Havant, Hampshire,
    Great Britain (U.S. Naval Observatory):
    39 r.
Striemann Photo: 50 b.
C. Titulaer: 164 r.
Universiteitsbibliotheek, Utrecht,
    Netherlands: 15
H. Roger Viollet: 11, 19 l.
ZEFA: 10, 66, 124, 126, 134, 155
All other illustrations: Evangelische
    Omroep, Hilversum, Netherlands (photos
    by Ko Durieux, Joop van der Elst, and
    Dolf Hoving).

*In the making of the photographs, we
received full cooperation from:*

American Museum of Natural History,
    New York: 88 l. and r., 90, 133 r.
Bowden, Malcolm: 119 t.l.
British Museum, London: 27 t., 28 l.,
    143, 145 l.
Dinosaur National Monument, Vernal,
    Utah: 89 r.
Downe House Estate and the Royal College
    of Surgeons of England: 18 c., 19 r.,
    71, 85 l., 127
Egyptian Museum, Cairo: 27 b., 29 r.
Rijksmuseum van Natuurlijke Historie,
    Leyden, Netherlands: 111 c. and r.